John McInnes

The New Pilgrims

Living as Christians in the technological society

Ronald N. Haynes  Publishers, Inc.

Palm Springs, California 92263

First USA Edition 1981
Ronald N. Haynes Publishers, Inc.
Palm Springs, California 92263

Library of Congress Catalog Card Number 81-83168
ISBN 0-88021-011-7 (previously 0-86760-002-0)

Printed in the United States of America

Originally published by
ALBATROSS BOOKS
P.O. Box 320, Sutherland
N.S.W. 2232, Australia

Contents

Introduction

Yesterday I was moved to tears while watching a film—a film about three groups of people who decided to live differently. They did this in order to follow more closely the teaching and example of Jesus. I cried in identity with the commitment, the agony and the effort they were giving to their calling. They were new pilgrims in our technological society.

I cry too, but differently, at the easy identity of the church at large with the world. I mean by "church" both individual members and corporate institutions. Often the identity is not wanton but unwitting, which makes me agonize the more over the urgency of taking a new look at the Christian life. As I understand the Bible, Christians are to be in the world but not of it. Yet today "in" has become "of", with barely a whisper being raised in protest—except when the whisper becomes a cry of self-righteous indignation over some well-publicized controversy.

Cages are meant to be unlocked

This book attempts to pinpoint a few of the major areas where the church conforms to society's values, thus losing its distinctive witness. But I don't want to be primarily concerned with detailed analysis or faultfinding. The church is culturally imprisoned, but examining the prison should be done only to plan escape. The goal is to find the true freedom God intended for the church, both individually and corporately—to unlock the cage of our bondage and find release. The book is therefore an appeal for both re-examination and change—for open-heart surgery rather than a Band-Aid.

If you, who have picked up this book, are a Christian, then what I write is particularly addressed to you because you are in a position to respond. You share my faith in God through Jesus Christ and the experience of the enabling power of the Holy Spirit. You are in the church and also in the world and you can bring about reform in both. If you are not a Christian, I hope you won't put the book down. I hope rather that you will be encouraged by what you read, to know that some Christians are unhappy about what has happened to the church and to society at large, and want both to change. I even dare hope that you will find here a glimpse of the Christian life as it can be and that you may, as a result, be drawn to consider becoming a disciple of Christ's yourself.

A style of life

Jacques Ellul, sociologist, lawyer and Christian thinker, speaking from France just after World War II, saw things correctly when he wrote:

> When we seek to discover effective action for the church owing to the necessity for its intervention in the world, it seems as though its first objective should be the creation of a style of life. For, if we consider the life of Christians in our churches, we see certainly that they make good sons, fathers, husbands, employers and workmen—"good, like good bread", said Aragon. They have many individual virtues, but

they have no style of life, or rather they have exactly that which has been imposed upon them by their sociological conditions, that is, by their social class, their nation, their environment and so on. It is not their spiritual condition which affects their style of life: it is their political or economic condition and, from this point of view, they are an overwhelming demonstration of the truth, temporary and temporal, of Marxism.[1]

And again when he said a few pages later:

. . . the whole of life is concerned . . . It includes the way we think about the present political questions, as well as our way of practicing hospitality. It also affects the way we dress and the food we eat . . . as well as the way in which we manage our financial affairs. It includes being faithful to one's wife as well as being accessible to one's neighbor. It includes the position one ought to take on current social and political questions, as well as the decisions which relate to the personal employment of our time . . . Absolutely everything, the smallest details of which we regard as indifferent, ought to be questioned, placed in the light of faith and examined from the point of view of the glory of God. It is on this condition that, in the church, we might possibly discover a new style of Christian life, voluntary and true.[2]

Where Ellul's remarks itch is at the level of everyday life. A friend, sitting with me on a commuter train journey, once commented:

"If I could ever see a church where Christians really care for people, where they weren't just materialists and where they really lived according

to Jesus' teaching and example, then I'd believe—
I'd become a Christian. But I don't think I ever
will. Churches are just institutions. I grew up in
one. I've even been on the church council. But its
meetings were just business meetings like any
others."

Now that's heavy criticism and it is said in one form or
another by thousands, not just as an excuse but truthfully.
We don't need to become pragmatists to see that example
and practical demonstration matter. Christians talk a lot
about "witness", the "fruits of the Spirit" and other New
Testament qualities, yet often the expectation of seeing those
qualities is confined to private, personal characteristics. Is
humility only the way I shyly smile? Could humility determine the sort of furniture in my house, the essential characteristic of relationships I have with my bosses and
subordinates in the factory where I work or, if I am a busi-
nessman, the real usefulness of what I market?

What a pity that so few took notice of what Ellul was
contending in 1949. He was talking about living in the kingdom in the world. He and others like him have been largely
ignored until recently. One reason for neglecting this plea
has been a fear that too concrete a prescription for Christian
living could itself become a new legalism. Jesus certainly
wasn't advocating that! Such fear is understandable and
helpful if it acts as a brake on the sort of teaching which
says, "Christians will spend no more than $5,000 per year
on themselves" or "Christians will own dogs weighing no
more than 20 lbs.". New pharisaical "thou shalt nots" we
don't want! But this legitimate fear should not stop us from
trying to understand and work out what being Christian
signifies right across the whole of life.

Another fear has been that the task of examining how we

live at home, at work and at church will distract us from the centrality of the Christian faith. "We must", it is said, "concentrate upon Christ and witness to him". Those of a conservative biblical orientation, who usually hold such a view have often pointed out that it is "liberals", "social gospellers", "Christian humanists" and various others who have been concerned with how to live, but for whom a supernatural God is dead or at least quite sick. "Be careful", it is said, "or you'll go the way they have gone". And that has deterred many Christians of a conservative theology from ever starting.

But labelling is a petty pastime, and such warnings are well-intentioned but easily misplaced. Indeed that attitude has a lot to answer for, because it prescribes a dangerously narrow definition of "witness" which seems to ignore the full implications of those sayings of Jesus which have a social and human dimension, sayings such as "By this all men will know that you are my disciples, if you have love for one another"[3] and "As you did it [a kind act] to one of the least of these brethren, you did it for me".[4] When asked by a lawyer what must be done to inherit eternal life, according to Luke's account Jesus replied:

> "What is written in the law? How do you read?" And he answered, "You shall love the Lord your God with all your heart, and with all your soul, and with all your strength, and with all your mind; and your neighbor as yourself." And he said to him, "You have answered right; do this, and you will live".[5]

And when asked to define "neighbor", Jesus told the story of the good Samaritan.[6] There is no doubt that the neighbor was the one up to his eyebrows *in* the world, not of it. Before the good Samaritan became involved, the institutional religious representatives walked on past. They were *of* the world, not in it.

But those at the other end of the theological scale have erred too. Some, who have seen relationships in the world as all important, have capitulated too easily to the norms currently prevailing in society. Such people see rightly that there are many irritable, bad relationships which need realignment and healing or injustices which need righting, but they don't always perceive that a fundamental critique is often necessary to isolate and then change that malady which is causing the irritation. All too often there has been an abandonment of a critical or prophetic stand which finds its base in the implications of being members of God's kingdom, the kingdom prevailing wherever God's rule is accepted.

I remember an industrial chaplain speaking reflectively about himself and like-minded colleagues of critical and liberal theological persuasion. He told me that, although he regards highly a lot of what he and his associates do and say, he fears that too easily they lose their "biblical taproot" from which springs their critique of industry and their distinctive ministry to people within it.

Christians are to be sojourning pilgrims[7] in this world, but very easily we become residents and citizens very much at home. Then we have nothing distinctive to contribute. When Asian students study and live in an overseas country such as New Zealand, they cannot put aside their cultural origins. They congregate to eat their own food, speak their own languages and be at ease with each other. Similarly citizens of God's kingdom are a little like foreigners. They identify with and respond to needs in the world, but are motivated from another set of circumstances and values and come together frequently. Nonetheless we all know what sometimes happens. The foreign student is so captivated by the culture in which he is studying that he totally identifies with it, loses his links with home and never wishes to go back. Uncomfortably, too often that's what happens to Christians in the world.

The life of the kingdom

What this book argues is that Christians, if they understand what it means to live in and for the kingdom, must see their loyalty to their king operating in all areas of life, including those which many of us have regarded as neutral and thus accepted as "the way it goes".

Although the task of finding a truly Christian style of living may seem too big to even begin, we can glean encouragement. Take my friend on the train. Two years later he *did* find a church which had within it a core of people who spoke and lived in such a way that he was able to say to himself, "It's real—I will!" He entered the "community of the forgiven" and found there both peace and challenge to a different way of being.

Perspectives

My direct experience is largely of the New Zealand scene. New Zealand is a pleasant-to-live-in, well-fed, somewhat self-satisfied small country at "the foot of the globe". But from what I have read, from what I have seen while traveling overseas, from reactions to snippets of this writing which have appeared before, the concerns of which I speak are present in all the so-called Western democracies . . . and in many places beyond.

Thanks

Many people have contributed to this book, some without

realizing that they have. Some of the subjects written about here have been discussed at times with senior students and graduates in various parts of the Tertiary Students Christian Fellowship (N.Z.) and others more recently with some of my colleagues and friends in the Interchurch Trade and Industry Mission (Wellington). Fellow members of my church, All Saints, Ngaio, have shared in my life in many ways over the last eight years and they, particularly the group of people with whom I live in community, have loved, provoked and stimulated me.

I especially want to thank Marion, my wife, for both her detailed work in checking text and footnotes and her encouragement over the whole project. I have also benefited from help and guidance from John Waterhouse of Albatross Books, with whom it has been a pleasure to work.

1
Time

I first thought seriously about time when waiting for some-one to open a luggage store. An Indian customs official, sitting with me in a stifling, vaporous Calcutta taxi, said as we frittered away the minutes and then the hours, "Why are you Westerners always so impatient—so much in a hurry?"

We commonly say:

> "There's no time."
> "If only I had more time."
> "Sorry I wasn't able to see you—time ran out."

Our predicament

Time seems to be severely measured. The watch on my wrist never pauses to catch a breath. Many of us, older and youn-ger, professionals and trades people, are rushing here and there, trying to fulfil a dozen obligations. Most people I meet are oppressed by time. It is either the study period, vaca-tions, the working week or the weekend, which is too short or too long, but never right.

"But at least we're not worried about time in the church."

Wrong. Here rushed timetables, too, are commonplace. Even as I was writing this paragraph I heard someone say in the office, "I'm always tired on Mondays—must be all the church activities on Sundays!"

The pressures of work, church, family, business expectations and a dozen other matters seem to make most of us time-sick. Must we be condemned to a life of unfinished tasks, unkept promises, unmet deadlines and endless frustration? Isn't there a better way? Is it to be found by going to the East and sitting on the banks of the Ganges?

I don't think so. There is often to be found a fatalism, a passivity that neglects the opportunities that time presents.

Time is one of the most fundamental frameworks in which we live. How should we look at time? What can Christians offer to our perception of time as a concept and a commodity?

Time by content

The Bible talks of time by its content rather than by its duration. It often speaks of "times" or "seasons" rather than time in the sense of hours and minutes. Thus there are times of evening, harvest, marriage, temptation, refreshing and so on.[1] There are also seasons, not only the climatic seasons of summer, autumn, winter and spring,[2] but seasons for rain, day and night, maturing in character, speaking an appropriate word and growing old.[3]

Even political events have their time and season. God, Daniel tells us, changes times and seasons by removing kings and setting up new regimes; while Jesus warned his disciples against trying to delve into the future and know the time and seasons for human history—events that are strictly in God's hands.[4]

Best known of all is the catalog of times and seasons in Ecclesiastes chapter 3 which begins, "For everything there is a season, and a time for every matter under heaven". This "matter" or "purpose" is given to man and he is to take the opportunity it contains. It is no use his doing the right thing at the wrong time. He has to understand the "given".

There is time to break down (to cast away stones) and a time to construct (to gather stones).[5] Moreover, because this age must be recognized for what it is—a period in which there is evil—there are times of hate, war and killing as well as times of love, peace and healing. Over it all God exercises a plan.

Even time-measurement words like "day" and "year", though sometimes straightforwardly chronological, frequently have a content flavor. For example, there is "the day of God's anger"[6] or "the year of recompense".[7] Indeed all the chronological terms such as "hour", "day", "at the time" and "moment" are a little fuzzy at the edges, as if exact measurement was not the main biblical concern. In fact even God seems muddled about what time is! "With the Lord one day is as a thousand years and a thousand years as one day."[8]

Neither the Old nor the New Testament say much about measured time. The New Testament does use *chronos* for measured time,[9] but seems more concerned with *kairos*[10] which carries the thrust of "time by opportunity and fulfilment". The opportunity is provided by God. Man's response is to fulfil the opportunity appropriately.

To use a simple example, a "time of harvest" is an opportunity to reap the crop, but a man has to take that opportunity, otherwise he gets nothing. God creates the opportunity, but we need to create the means for its fulfilment.

Is the concern for "time by content" rather than "time by measurement" simply reflective of a primitive age when measuring systems were not accurate? Certainly the sophistication of time devices makes us more conscious of chronology, but there is another factor. The Bible sees God as acting in time, while yet beyond time. All events, whether natural or man-made history, are his. For instance, God feeds all living creatures "in due season"[11] or Jeremiah thunders forth of "the time of the Lord's vengeance".[12]

> *This designation of time by its content is characteristic of the whole biblical tradition, and is concerned with the understanding of time realistically "in terms of opportunity and fulfilment".*[23]

Time delineated by its content is not a theological idea found only by drawing together word studies from Old and New Testament—although that's part of it. Jesus himself thrillingly exemplified the same understanding in his own life.

When Jesus had been called to Jairus' daughter, he stopped on the way and healed a woman. He gave that woman the full measure of time needed to meet her needs—in this case only a few minutes. And then he still went on to his prior task, secure that he was able to do both.[14] Thus he was not bustled into a mad chronology. Content gave meaning to duration. Content often determined duration. What he did fitted appropriately with the length of time the particular task demanded. Schedules as such didn't rule.

Let us take some more examples. Look at Jesus' dispute with his brothers. Although he finally went to the festival at Judea, he did not do so because of his family's urging. "My time (*kairos*) has not yet fully come",[15] he told them. He went later, but only because to do so fitted with God's timetable. He frequently gave hours to people where there was a fruitful ministry. The Samaritan woman at the well and her family took hours . . . and then two days.[16] Or again, he took night hours for prayer because the occasion before or after those nights demanded it.[17]

Jesus could cry from the cross after three short years of ministry, which often included exhausting work, "It is finished"[18]—when it wasn't. At least, the need for the healing and teaching was not finished, but he had kept his father's timetable and thus his work really was completed. Other agencies (the church and the Holy Spirit) were now to carry on. Finished it was too, because each specific ministry which had come his way had been dealt with. Each task was given the time it deserved.

Bullying time

To biblical authors—and to Jesus as the supreme example— the passage of time was not a frustration, a curse or an embarrassment, but for today's man frequently it is (though at times it can be an advantage to get something unpleasant over and done with). Christians, like everyone else, tend to bully, push or manipulate time, trying to pack in more and more activities. We think we can overcome our frustration at time's passing by constantly reordering priorities and improving our efficiency.

I know people who dream up impossible work schedules, and others who think out to the second which route is the fastest, which lane saves the most time, and who then get great joy from arriving fifty-four seconds earlier than by the alternative way! "Bullying time" is a denial of time's God-given nature.

"Faster faster"

Time seems to be something that we perpetually want to beat. Sure, one can thrill to the challenge of a champion athlete like John Walker running 2,000 meters in four minutes 51.4 seconds before a Norwegian crowd. There's a real achievement in slicing 4.8 seconds off an exceptional ten-year-old record.

But this athletic thrill that we get by doing or watching doesn't mean that we must transfer a "faster faster" attitude to every aspect of life. In the end, "faster faster" is a futile quest because there is an absolute limit, even if that limit is not yet known.

The money-makers

Many Christians are in the profit-and-loss business, where the pressure to conform to the view that "time is money" is strong. It screams with insistent urgency at us. "Quick thinkers", we are persuaded in a full-page advertisement in *Time* magazine, "use the Fly-Drive Service, because it saves time, and time is money. [It] . . . makes short work of long hours". This type of persuasion is regarding time not by its content but by productivity.

Why is productivity so important? We should not succumb to a biased and decidedly materialistic perversion of the stewardship of time. Such a view makes greater and greater production the goal for which to strive, on the false assumption that "more and more" is equivalent to "better and better" and the value of any task can be strictly measured by the time it takes. Preoccupation and productivity ignores or betrays the importance of "time by content" and especially "time by people content".

The time-savers

Saving time is equally a snare and a delusion. What right have we to try to save something which is designed by its Creator to pass away? The very passage of time is a security for us. Thus writing this book demands many hours and these hours belong to that writing—not to something else. Because the writing calls for this time, I can cheerfully say

"No" to other thing which badger me for my attention.

The question I really have to resolve is whether or not the writing itself deserves to be part of my life at present. Moreover, when writing-time is finished, I should be free to move cheerfully on without looking back over my shoulder to worry about the way I have spent my time. We need not wonder, "Was it worth it?"

The monument builders

Another heresy pokes its nose in here. This is monument-making. Have you noticed our tendency to leave monuments to our efforts? To make our mark, to have it said that our work "put the church on a new track", is a wonderful thing —or is it? This attitude is very common in professional circles. A man works hard to put his stamp upon a business and might even be remembered by the erection of a memorial to his name. In family life we desire sons so that our family name may be perpetuated.

What we're really trying to do is to make the time-limited or earth-bound, timeless or eternal. Put another way, we can say that we are trying to make permanent the temporary. We are viewing things from a man-centered perspective. The theocentric has become egocentric.

It is true that our language hasn't totally lost the idea of "time by content". We say "breakfast time", "exam time", "holidays", "Christmas time" and so on, and have no difficulty picturing those periods quite concretely in terms of both the activities and the emotion attached to them. But that's not the overriding emphasis of our societies. We are much more concerned with measured time, such as when we work or play to the umpire's whistle. Moreover even in most descriptions of "time by content" which we habitually use, there is no mention or consciousness of God, whereas the biblical view is quite sure that both commonplace occurrences and extraordinary happenings are directly from God.

Living in God's time

Recovering the notion that events are God-given will result in us having more time to worship, pray, adore and praise. Modern Christians often lament their difficulty in finding time to be with God. Taken together, the shortage of time and society's materialistic outlook work against prayer—activity constantly demands preoccupation with itself. But if we are highly conscious that God gave "the time", might we not more easily acknowledge him? That acknowledgement can be a very practical help to one who is spasmodic in prayer, worried about not keeping time with God and ineffective in finding remedies.

Time, whether for operating a machine, gardening, Christian fellowship or anything else, becomes "his" as well as "mine"! Therefore the notion of praising him at all times[19] becomes part of whatever we are doing, rather than a disruptive intrusion into our main daily activity. If we learn to be aware of living in God's times, we can then praise him for the opportunity each moment presents.

Which way around?

Instead of organizing our days, hours or weeks by saying explicitly or by default, "Now here's some time—what do we put in it and what are our priorities?" we could start at the other end. Each of us can say instead, "Here are the important things that I need to enter into—my study or work, my family, and my local church. Now what opportunities do they present and how do I respond to or fulfil those opportunities?" Or "What season am I in? How much time should be bound up with each activity if it is to be done to God's glory?"

Decision-making is not avoided. We still need prayer and the indwelling presence of God's Holy Spirit in our lives demonstrating the things we need to do—perhaps more so. But what we are doing is paralleling in our own lives the biblical emphasis that time is primarily determined by God-given content.

Drifting goes, too. I can't see time as neutral anymore, a mere abstraction in which I live. God holds it in his hands. It is a part of his creation into which I need to fit.

Saying "No!"

We will say "No" more often. Suppose, for instance, that I am a student. "Student days" for me are a time of preparation. What I *learn* both formally and informally while being a student much more characterizes what we call "student days" than does the actual *length* of my course. Some people have one year, some have five, but all can talk meaningfully about "student days" because the emphasis is upon content.

If I believe in God's sovereignty, then I know that my academic and professional training is in God's plan, integrated with other parts of my life such as my church, my life in some student or work-orientated fellowship, my emancipation from my mother and father and so on. Because "student days" are a time of preparation to which I am called by God, I'll give myself to that, knowing that I can safely say "No" to many demands which are not now appropriate.

So if it is suggested that I be a youth leader, I must ask "Does it fit?" I should not ask "Is there time?" If it fits, it belongs to my time of preparation—it belongs to my student days and it must receive the time it requires. I have to come to this question from the right way around, otherwise I will miss God's guidance. If I am having to steal time to give to something, that "something" is seriously awry and I should not be part of it.

Suppose I am now employed full-time, as well as being a parent of young children. I know that my family is the prime responsibility. The years until the children leave home should be primarily devoted to family life. I can therefore safely put aside extra professional and voluntary work, tempting as it may be, which impinges on these "family years".

The extra things which make demands may be wonderful in themselves, but are they part of the content of the time that I am presently in? I must be wary of the appeal, "Ah, but there's such need", or "Oh, you're so good at it". If it's not part of my time at the moment, then that activity is not for me. We need not feel guilty. These other (legitimate) responsibilities are not at present God's task for us.

One time becomes another. For instance, when people carry into marriage priorities that were right before but which do not belong to the new time, trouble brews. If the prime time is "beginning marriage", but the job is tearing the marriage apart at the seams, there's something wrong with the job. And the same can be said of many other aspects of life. I need to know that any given time is a *kairos*, a time of opportunity and fulfilment for me, set apart primarily for the purpose for which it's been designated. Everything else must fit into that, not burst it apart.

I have felt the force of that pressure and fought it myself. Three or four years ago I had to halve a business trip of several weeks and cancel a smaller one because the disarray at home was too great. I misread the time I was in. I was caught up by work expectations. A young family in a new city demanded my being at home, not careering around the countryside seeing people. My job had extended beyond its appropriate time.

For the same reason I've found myself saying "No" to more than a self-determined minimum of evening meetings. And what a benefit that's been proven to be. Moreover I have discovered that other people understand my point of view and appreciate the fact that someone is prepared to stand firm. What is also interesting is that time and again my saying "No" has cleared the way for others to make their contribution.

Natural times

Another implication concerns comfort and convenience. Once we see that times and seasons in the more descriptive literal sense (e.g. winter clothes), as well as time in the more spiritual sense (e.g. a time of repentance) are given by God, we will also realize that in the modern West men try to defeat or bypass many of these allocated times. Ready-made examples are commonplace.

Deep freezers and central heating are used to turn winter into summer. Might we not be healthier and certainly use less energy in an energy-hungry and energy-disparate world, if winter clothes replaced a few degrees of interior house warmth? Would it be too silly to be much more accepting of seasonal ebb and flow, scarcity and glut, in fruit and vegetables rather than store them by cooling, freezing or some other energy-consuming method?

I know that such suggestions are often dismissed as the views of health food fadists or environmentalists who have gone too far. Or they're dismissed as advocating a romantic, primitivistic call back to nature. But we should not make such excuses. Such questions and their answers follow directly from taking seriously a view of times or seasons as God-given. They force us to think about acquiescing to habits in our society which are so germane to it that we have accepted them without critique. Heating a building and using abundant natural growth in one season to cover scarcity in another have always been part of man's endeavor, and it may be argued that such activities spring from both man's creative abilities and the biblical mandate to be steward over other created things. But there is also a point at which that must stop before it become ruthless greed—a symptom of man's getting out of touch with God and being at war with his environment. The biblical doctrine of everything having a time and season is a corrective to such tendencies which are rife in our world.

George

The story of George brings to a crunch the application of "time by content". George, when I worked with him, was principal of a well-known institution. From his biblical study and close contact with a missionary working in a Third World village culture, he came to realize that he and his family were living in sin—the sin of affluence—and so he, his wife and children decided that they must repent.

They realized that repentance is not "saying sorry and keeping on doing it", but a lengthy period of turning to God in sorrow for forgiveness. It involves putting right the wrong, with the intention of treading new paths in the future. Therefore they entered a two year "time of repentance". They sold their large house in a prestigious suburb and moved to a smaller one. They swapped their energy-hogging car for a small model. They examined their food, decided they were guilty of gross over-eating, cut down their food intake and improved the quality of their diet. George lost forty pounds. Money saved was given away.

Those sorts of moves weren't easy. They were thought to be a little strange. People of his status didn't do that! But with help and support from a small group of perceptive friends, George and his family stuck to it. When I met him, the time of repentance had about four months to run and George was wondering what God would lead them into next.

The time of Christ

We have not finished with the biblical view. In the New Testament the concept of time is supremely worked out in Christ. With the birth of Jesus, the time of Christ has begun, as forecast in the Old Testament, and this is the time of opportunity for people to turn to him. John Marsh, a biblical scholar, puts it this way:

> The kairos, *initiated by the birth of Jesus, is not yet closed. The day of opportunity is still here and we in the twentieth century can use the* now *of the divine redemptive present with the New Testament writers. The* chronos, *the duration of the* kairos, *is not yet run out.* [20]

To accept Jesus as Lord and Savior is to respond affirmatively to this opportunity. For the person who has become a Christian there is a constant command to present the opportunity to others. The fact that we are in the time of Christ is a spur to sharing the gospel and this sharing is to color any other time which we are in.

So in our student days or family years, or any smaller times such as exam time or lunch hour, we will feel the biting urgency of opening this opportunity of salvation to others. This opening and sharing will never be an "extra" but always an interwoven part of the nitty-gritty of daily living. We don't need to go seeking people. There will be a ring of them all around us as we move through the day. An understanding that we live in this time of Christ enables us to enfold specific biblical commands such as "be his witnesses",[21] "preach in season and out of season",[22] and "be the salt of the earth"[23] within the compass of our whole being. We do not have to see such commands as unhappy conscience-pricking intrusions or special evangelistic efforts. They belong in our lives as do stones on a beach.

This age and God's kingdom now

Another lesson emerges as we feel the force of the biblical teaching about "ages". The Greek word *aion*, frequently used in the New Testament, should be translated "age". The New Testament distinguishes "this age"[24] from the "the age to come".[25]

"This age", which lasts from creation until the return of Christ, is the age in which the force of Satan's rule is to be felt.[26] In it, since the events of the fall recorded in Genesis chapter 2, temptation, sin, pain and imperfection abound. Into "this age" has come with the birth, death and resurrection of Jesus, power from the future of God's reign.[27] *That* is the age in which God's kingdom, rule, sovereignty or authority will be supreme. That kingdom is also called eternal life.[28] The amazing news Jesus brought was that those who follow him could, in *this* age, begin to live as if they were in the age to come.[29] Resources of his power through the Holy Spirit were made available to those who accepted him in repentance and thus were forgiven their sins.

So there is an overlapping or intermingling of ages. The new age infiltrates the present by a kind of spiritual osmosis. To the extent to which people understand the life, death and resurrection of Christ and accept that meaning for themselves, to that extent the kingdom is present in this age.

So it is that the discussion of time leads us to the kingdom of God. His kingdom is both future and present. In the preaching and life of Jesus, linear time scales are superseded. Those who follow Jesus can now take part, albeit imperfectly, in a life, a relationship, a set of values and a motivation that are derived from "the age to come". For Christians to live any other way is to betray their citizenship in God's kingdom:

> *Their life is thus perpetual tension between a present which is potentially closed and a future which is already present. They must live in the present age without giving their hearts to it.*[30]

A related tension occurs in employment where the expectations of employer or fellow employees are sometimes at odds with those of the individual Christian. Conflict is almost inevitable because of the different values held. An employer is likely to be unimpressed by someone who says, "Because I have a Christian view of time, I cannot do all that overtime work this month". But what is often recognized by employers is the wisdom of giving time to family, time to recreation or time to socially benefitting organizations. The Christian's view of time helps reinforce the conviction that his decision to give prime time to his family, or whatever it is, is right. It gives him confidence in standing firm when criticized for departing from the accepted standard.

These conflicts and tensions are things to which we will return in later chapters. It's enough now to come to grips with what we might call "kingdom time". By becoming Christians we begin to participate now in eternity. Linear concepts of time are inadequate to cope with this idea. We must hold firmly to "time by content", time according to God's priorities for us as people. The danger is that conditioning by society's time scales and values can easily crush the influence of "the age to come", even though we have by believing already entered it.

Time and the church

But we now need to relate time to the doctrine of the church as the body of Christ, because it is in the context of church that the biblical concepts of the time make sense.

> Rustle, bustle, skid and scrape.
> Help! Look out! I'm running late.
> If *I'm* not there, what will they do?
> Who could substitute for me? Not *you!*

Unwarranted self-importance often surges to the surface. All too easily an individual places himself center stage. It's so nice to have someone say, "He's a fantastic worker in the church. He does everything. He never spares himself. He's on fire for the Lord!" This is common mispraise. It's measuring spirituality by activity. It leads to an emphasis on meetings and projects, rather than a focus on corporate life together in which the fruits of the Spirit show themselves.

In a local church, hands and eyes, feet and legs—all the different people with their variety of gifts—need to be allowed to work.[31] All too frequently too few do too much, thus going beyond their appointed functions. In a corporate fellowship, intimate believers should be able to help each other determine what "time" each is in and therefore what priorities must be adopted.

Moreover, what has been said about individuals or families can be said about churches. A local church has always as its mandate to glorify God and be his people, his light and his love, and to proclaim his message. But how can it know what it should be concentrating upon at any time? Many churches either drift, or follow traditional patterns of activities. But if the parish church is convinced, for example, that "now" is its "time of repentance", then its emphasis and activities over the next few months could be designed to strip itself of its worldliness by letting those things which have become useless disappear and by ridding itself of excess possessions that hang around its neck.

Another parish, convinced it was in "a time of sacrificial service", would give itself unremittingly to showing Christian love by visiting and helping in the new housing estate, in the railway settlement or among seasonal workers coming into the district.

And how would it know its time? By discerning what was going on in the world around it, by listening to those in its fellowship with the gifts of prophecy and by spending time corporately in prayer with the express purpose of finding out. Wouldn't that be marvellous? To know one's time in this way would lift the common life of the local church beyond the routine, the spasmodic or the whims of a few into the realm of corporate, convinced action. "It seemed good to the Holy Spirit and to us."[32] Few churches that I know behave like that, but the one or two that do have always had a great sense of divine mission.

The quiet revolution

We cannot claim more than is due for a biblical understanding of time, applied individually and corporately. It is not a magic formula. Nevertheless, living within a concept of time determined by God's kingdom will bring its own quiet revolution. On becoming Christians we enter a different time framework. We are no longer contained by, nor preoccupied with, a human scale with its perimeter points of birth and death. Nor do our values remain the same.

If we only have the human scale, then events such as starting and leaving school, going to college or university, getting married, commencing work, becoming a foreman or boss, having children, then grandchildren, becoming president of the Rotary or even an elder in the church are the main milestones and target points of life. Because eternity's time scale and the presence of God's kingdom invade us, there come among these human events other milestones and targets such as learning to commune with God in prayer without distraction, seeing our church become a group of disciples or showing such selfless love to each other that others recognize it as distinctive. These kinds of milestones and targets are less obviously measureable at any point of time, but they will (or will not!) become quite apparent as the years pass by.

As we say "No" more frequently to demands for our involvement in myriad activities, so will others who have the same understanding and thus many activities will die. And that will be good. "Being" will have a chance to triumph over "doing". "Meeting" will come before "meetings".

Both individuals and groups need to recover the notion that time passes and it is right for it to do so. Therefore we won't need to be thinking in terms of permanence, but in terms of things appropriate to their own time. The essence of the gospel is permanently the same, but not the cultic incrustations. Thus when we build buildings, arrange committees or establish institutions, we will know that they are useful only for a limited period. They can be tailor-made to our requirements and can fade away when their work is finished.

We will be able to enjoy any appointed time, whatever it is, for what it is. We will be able to rejoice in doing less and doing it better, safe in the knowledge that others will be doing their part because we are all in the body of Christ. We will be stimulated by the knowledge, too, that the time allocated to a particular task is to be fully utilized, thus fulfilling the God-given opportunity inherent in the job itself. And we will be aware that for everyone the main time of opportunity is that of responding to Jesus Christ.

The phrase "alternative lifestyle" hangs on many lips these days. Whether they use the term or not, many people are looking for an alternative to the strains and tensions of modern Western materialism. A re-orientation of how to think about time is one of the fundamental alternatives which Christians can offer to society at large. Time is not a prison: it is a God-given opportunity.

2
Simplicity

Possessions have become our social yardstick. We value a man and give a person status according to the extent of his wealth. Yet contrast this with the teaching of Jesus: "A man's life does not consist in the abundance of his possessions".[1]

Martin Pawley, a modern social commentator, writes:

> *Consumer goods today determine social realities; they are the only reliable guide to income, lifestyle and aspirations . . . Do you own a car, a central heating system, a clothes drier, a dish washer, a shaver, an electric blanket, an electric cooker, an electric iron, an electric kettle, an electric floor polisher, an electric food and drink mixer, a gas cooker, a gas or electric refrigerator, a hair drier, a household radio, a record player, electric space heaters, gas space heaters, oil or paraffin space heaters, a tape recorder, a television set, an electric toaster, a vacuum cleaner, a washing machine, an electric toothbrush? Do you have a bank account, credit cards, investments? All these things fit in and around your home, which has become a kind of consumer envelope for the purpose.*[2]

If Pawley is right—even half right—then in fact people's lives in the wealthy West do "consist in the abundance of their possessions". What we will discuss in this chapter is how Christians can live in such societies, yet honor the teachings Jesus gave about the things we possess.

Crucial Jesus teaching

Consider Luke 12:13–34 which, together with the parallel passage in Matthew 6:19–34, explains Jesus' attitude to possessions. It's worth reading in full. As translated in the *New English Bible,* it reads:

> 13A man in the crowd said to him, "Master, tell my brother to divide the family property with me". 14He replied, "My good man, who set me over you to judge or arbitrate?" 15Then he said to the people, "Beware! Be on your guard against greed of every kind, for even when a man has more than enough, his wealth does not give him life". 16And he told them this parable: "There was a rich man whose land yielded heavy crops. 17He debated with himself: 'What am I to do? I have not the space to store my produce. 18This is what I will do', said he. 'I will pull down my storehouses and build them bigger. I will collect in them all my corn and other goods, 19and then say to myself, *Man, you have plenty of good things laid by, enough for many years: take life easy, eat, drink, and enjoy yourself.'* 20But God said to him, 'You fool, this very night you must surrender your life; you have made your money—who will get it now?' 21That is how it is with the man who amasses wealth for himself and remains a pauper in the sight of God." 22Therefore", he said to his disciples, "I bid you put away anxious thoughts about food to keep you alive and clothes to cover your body. 23Life is more

than food, the body more than clothes. 24Think of
the ravens: they neither sow nor reap; they have
no storehouse or barn; yet God feeds them. You
are worth far more than the birds! 25Is there a man
among you who by anxious thought can add a foot
to his height? 26If, then, you cannot do even a very
little thing, why are you anxious about the rest?
27Think of the lilies: they neither spin nor weave;
yet I tell you, even Solomon in all his splendor was
not attired like one of these. 28But if that is how
God clothes the grass, which is growing in the field
today, and tomorrow is thrown on the stove, how
much more will he clothe you! How little faith you
have! 29For all these are things for the heathen to
run after; but you have a Father who knows that
you need them. 31No, set your mind upon his kingdom, and all the rest will come to you as well.
32"Have no fear, little flock; for your Father has
chosen to give you the kingdom. 33Sell your possessions and give in charity. Provide for yourselves
purses that do not wear out, and never-failing treasure in heaven, where no thief can get near it, no
moth destroy it. 34For where your wealth is, there
will your heart be also."

Taking this and the Matthew passage together, three main
points demand attention, namely "seek the kingdom",
"beware of greed" and "store up treasure in heaven".

Seek the kingdom

Jesus says you are "not to set your mind on food and drink"
(verse 29), but you are to "set your mind on his kingdom,
and all the rest will come to you as well" (verse 31). The
extreme primacy of this command to "seek his kingdom"

must be really appreciated. This is not just "a first", but "the first".

The immediate corrective to giving possessions too great a place in our lives is not to reorganize the possessions, but to go back to the prime life-motive of concentrating on God. Obtaining, maintaining and overvaluing possessions will only then slip down the scale of our priorities.

The "all the rest" is important. As the passage makes clear, the phrase means food, clothes and drink, representing the essentials for personal living. Sometimes preachers understand that phrase symbolically, to stand not just for essentials, but everything we have in the culture in which we live. Thus all consumer goods, transport, holidays, complex architecture and lots more would be included. If this meaning is accepted, then the emphasis tends to move from "set your mind upon the kingdom" to "all the rest", because "all the rest" is so appealing. And sometimes even the emphasis is allowed to fall upon "all", with the notion that the more a person sets his mind on the kingdom, the more things he is entitled to get! Thus abundance becomes a *reward* for obedience.

Such a view however does violence to the context of this verse and to the style of life Jesus himself lived. Food and clothes are "needs" because God sees them that way. They are not luxuries over and beyond our regular necessities. The needs which God promises to meet stand in emphatic contrast to the warning "do not store up treasure on earth" and the declaration about "the man who amasses wealth for himself and remains a pauper in the sight of God". And that comment follows the strident parable of the rich fool who hoarded to no purpose. No! Jesus is not talking about rewards and abundance at all. The emphasis falls on "seek first the kingdom", not on "all the rest"—let alone upon "all"!

Jesus is giving first a command and then a reassurance,

especially to a timid follower, that giving priority to living under God's rule (for that is what "kingdom" means) will not result in physical destitution. Although, unlike non-believers, the follower of Jesus will not deliberately "seek all these things", he will not be abandoned. God is just. That is why Matthew remembers Jesus as saying that we are to set our minds upon God's justice as well as his rule.

And how will "all the rest" be provided? We will see later that usually it comes from wages, when a person works in accordance with the biblical teaching about work,[3] or from others, as Christians live in both the local and worldwide church, drawn in the New Testament as a compassionate, mutual responsibility society.[4] But we should not limit God's providing to those ways, because these passages at least leave the answer mysteriously in the Father's knowledge.

Beware of greed

The second point is highlighted by verse 15, which reads "Beware! Be on your guard against greed of every kind". Then follows, "for even when a man has more than enough, his wealth does not give him life", which is the *New English Bible* translation of the saying with which this chapter began. As a corollary to that are the words, "For where your treasure is, there will your heart be also".

Jesus is warning that, if we value possessions highly, our main affection and loyalty will be attached to them. As we shall see again, many features of our societies take on their own dynamic[5] and possessions are not exception. They constitute a powerful force in modern life. They become an authority, a power:

"I couldn't live like that; I couldn't do without . . ."
"Oh, no, we can't go. I can't bear to leave the

house after all the work and money we've put into
it."

"I feel too cut off without a TV. Whatever else we
do without, let's save up for *that*."

"I must have one of those. We're the only people
on the block who haven't got one."

All of this is commonplace talk. Possessions determine action.

For Christians the question of authority—what determines action—is crucial. Our authority is the Lord whom we serve, who died for our sin and set us free. We are to follow his example and his teaching as we live in his kingdom now, in this world. If some things usurp that authority, we are in trouble. Could it be that because possessions so dictate our lives we are often in practice living under a contrary authority, even while mouthing Christian words?

It is just at this point that so many of us come to grief. How easy it is to live "a life of faith", telling ourselves that we are concentrating on seeking first the kingdom of God, while knowing that if this faith-life fails, then we still have stored up somewhere an abundance which will carry us through. Like Rachel in the Old Testament or the shrewd primitive of New Guinea, we back both horses and keep our household gods tucked firmly in our saddlebag or hidden in the corner.

Further, if we are honest, we will probably know that we devote a lot of time and energy to ensuring that this abundance is adequately secure—in property, insurance, shares or loans. And if we are students about to begin a career, then it's highly likely that we too will soon begin to work ardently towards similar securities. The lofty ideals of an externally imposed poverty quickly give way when we start to make money.

Making provision for the near future or for others is not denied by Scripture. As an example for the wise, the ant is praised for storing food to preserve the life of its community.[6] And Paul tells Timothy to make sure people provide for their families.[7] Nor is thought about the future wrong. We are not to worry . . . but we are to think. Indeed we are asked to reflect deeply about how the birds and the flowers fare. They do well by staying with the source of food provided. The bird blown off course away from the sort of food it eats, or a seedling which grows on dry impoverished ground, dies. Likewise Christians need to stay with Christ and the people of his kingdom.

The false premise inherent in our trust in such securities is that we expect them not God to provide for us, and at a standard of living which we currently experience. That, for most of us, is a long way beyond the "needs" level.

Hence the securities must be large, expensive and worrying. We need more and more money to sustain them and the circle of excess is self-perpetuating.

Is it not self-evident that most of us, by following the prevailing pattern of society as urged by advertising and example (not least by the example of other Christians), have moved a long way from the plain instructions of Jesus? Is not the heart of our identification with today's culture challenged by the command "set your minds on the kingdom of God"? Are we not guilty of gross self-indulgence?

Store up treasure in heaven

Third, there is in verse 33 positive instruction to "provide for yourselves never-failing wealth in heaven" or, as more traditional translations have it, "store up treasure in heaven". That means to be and do what pleases God—to increase our experience of him and of his people. Christian disciples are to establish such a relationship with God, and consequently such a set of values for living, that material wealth, affluence or accumulation ceases to be important. In any case material security is so tenuous, so likely to suffer from damage, disrepair and loss or be made irrelevant by death, that it is only time wasting and anxiety producing. Christian people need to open their eyes and see again that simple reality and recapture something of its dynamic in their lives.

This relationship, once established, is to be cultivated. Jesus assumed prayer and fasting to be important and gave instruction about how they are to take place.[8] And that instruction emphasizes inward realities, while condemning flamboyancy towards others. Certain values have been commended, too-values like meekness, mercy and peacemaking as taught in the Beatitudes.[9] All those values and that essential relationship with God are eternal. They are attractive now because they bypass all possession-centered value systems and social structures, and they prepare us for life with God forever—unlike the grass described in verse 28, burned when it has finished its useful seedbearing.

A puzzle

It is precisely here that we get into a puzzling problem referred to in another way in the *Introduction*. We must grapple now with it more deliberately. If we conclude our discussion at this point, we are still left with questions like: "What is selfish accumulation?" "What does *essential* mean?" or "What does this alternative way of living look like?"

If we carry on and try to describe what Christian life should look like, we end all too easily in legalism—a set of rules and prescriptions about sizes of houses, calorific content of food, depth of carpet pile, numbers of electric kitchen helps, percentages of income to give away . . . and a multitude of other particulars. And if we don't immediately end in rules, we so concentrate on particular examples that they become first models and then, in the end, rules again.

The difficulty can be illustrated by glancing at two books, which helped start the (minor) waterfall of writing about Christian simplicity since 1971.

Vernard Eller, in *The Simple Life*, colorfully refused to paint a specific picture of the Christian's simple life. Not for him that "can of worms".[10] He stays at the level of "the theological and spiritual dynamics of Christian simplicity".[11] His adverse critics thus find him furiously frustrating because of his lack of practicality.

By contrast Art Gish, in *Beyond the Rat Race*,[12] plunges in at the other end. His wife, who shares the life which authenticates her husband's writing, discusses in the Foreword whether or not he should be particular, admits the dangers, then decides he should accept them. That sets the author on course for telling us all about going free to concerts, using second-hand paper and a whole host of other things. His adverse critics laugh at him for being so silly. The particulars become the memory points beyond which many readers do not pass.

Both authors in fact do provocatively good service. However their two approaches exemplify a difficulty which extends beyond them as writers and which poses a dilemma for each individual Christian or any Christian group. If we are to live out a simple life as taught by Jesus, must we not set some criteria? And how do we do that without becoming trendy Pharisees?

Another puzzle

As if that difficulty were not prickly enough, another closely related problem looms. We can illustrate it by referring to a modern anti-affluence Christian author. Ronald Sider wrote *Rich Christians in an Age of Hunger* [13] on the question of Christians and affluence at the levels of personal lifestyle, church life and of the structures of secular society. He does a lot of biblical and sociological examination before making some practical suggestions in the last third of the book.

Many New Zealand friends of mine were so moved in their minds and emotions at what he had already uncovered, applied and suggested that they were ready to do great things, but were then left feeling rather flat by his practical advice for individuals. The end point reached by many of these suggestions is the level at which most New Zealanders *start* before they read the book!

By world standards, North America and New Zealand are both affluent, but there are differences. Many New Zealanders, like many Australians and Europeans, find themselves already living below the North American standard of living, for example in the amount of energy consumed or the number of household gadgets used. In terms of direct material equivalents, they have already achieved the simplicity of lifestyle Sider suggests. Does this mean that they are therefore free of the same spirit of acquisitiveness that blights North American society? By no means!

The principles of simple lifestyle need to be worked out in the context of our own culture. We cannot lightly excuse ourselves because we are not starting on a par with a wealthier society. Although materially poorer, we may still be bound by the same greed, selfishness and preoccupation with material possessions.

Once, when I was discussing these matters with an international group, an Indian Christian leader said that Indians have similar problems. A villager striving to own a portable radio as a status symbol was in exactly the same situation as many affluent Westerners: he was tempted by the power of things. Clearly, any move towards living simply must be culturally anchored—but how? Are there no distinguishing marks of a simple lifestyle, whatever culture we happen to belong to?

In the direction of simplicity

Contained in the same crucial passage (Luke 12) are some other points. Jesus says in verses 32–33:

> *Have no fear, little flock, for your Father has chosen to give you the kingdom. Sell your possessions and give in charity.*

Phillips translates the latter part of that verse, "Give the money away". If this instruction is understood as a continual imperative—something to be done all through life—then the pattern of Christian simplicity begins to show quite powerfully. "Sell and give" is both a check upon accumulation and a positive instruction. All disciples are to have little, but share much.

"Less and less" rather than "more and more" therefore becomes the direction for our lives. It goes right against what is in vogue. As we "sell and give", setting our minds upon the kingdom, we will reverse the growth to bigger and bigger houses which hold more and more things as we go through life.

Asceticism is not being advocated, nor is primitivism. We will care for our children but we won't be tempted at the drop of a hat to add the extra room for "the kids to play in", or obey the advertisement which says to young couples that they need not put off buying "that piece of furniture that would look so well in the den", because "they could talk to the bank about it". This instruction of Jesus acts as a selector to eliminate some things, but choose others from every range of possibilities encountered in any area of life.

This idea of going in the direction of simplicity is linked with growing more and more closely to God's will. The more a person is influenced by God's holiness, justice and forgiveness, the less he will be dependent upon the temporary securities and vacuous status given by having many possessions. Only as one is more and more absorbed in God's calling is the life of simple, amiable nonconformity even possible.

In the personal area, owning fewer clothes, eating less expensive food and having simpler furnishings are three examples of the changes which will occur. Going this way will certainly constitute nonconformity, because that's the opposite of the usual pattern. These changes in what are only trivia of life will nevertheless gradually mark out the Christian as being "a bit different".

But the reverse is also true. If Christians do not show evidence of going in these directions, onlookers—and there are always many—will rightly wonder whether or not the Christians are serious about following God, because in externals they seem to conform ever so prettily to an avaricious pattern of society, and hence to its real values. Christians generally accumulate "more and more" all through life, just like everyone. Surely that means they have the same values as everybody else!

Cultural baggage, lambs and wolves

It is significant to ask if Christian simplicity is totally expressed by having fewer and less luxurious things, where "things" stands for the hundreds of possessions which litter our lives. Clearly, few possessions is a key idea in Jesus' expression of simplicity. His life, as far as we know, was in line with his teaching. There is no evidence that he had an elaborate inventory of goods and chattels to keep him independent as he moved about Palestine for three years. Instead he accepted hospitality gladly where it was offered.[14] We notice that both the twelve and the seventy disciples, when sent on their missions of proclamation, were told by Jesus to travel lightly. The seventy were instructed, "Carry no purse, no bag, no sandals and salute no one on the road".[15]

Here, in this last phrase, something else emerges. How strange that Jesus should instruct his disciples, who were to love and heal, that they were to greet no one on the way! But in those times greetings or salutations were far more than "Hello-goodby". The disciples were not to be distracted from their purpose by elaborate Eastern hospitality at every oasis or village. They were to cut through all that cultural baggage—in order to carry out their mission.

The directness exhibited here is an element of simplicity. It is demonstrated by the paradoxical entry into Jerusalem when Jesus rode only on an ass[16] although, as a king, he might have mounted a splendidly decorated thoroughbred. It shows also in his willingness to meet need by healing on the Sabbath day,[17] even when that broke contemporary expectations. It emerges again in the praise he gave to the tax collector who prayed "God be merciful to me a sinner",[18] as compared with the elaborate prayer of the Pharisee. Symbols—bread, wine, leaven, spit, coins, fig trees, the sower[19] and many more—Jesus certainly used a great deal, especially in answering questions. One might concede that such teaching was not direct. But that is poetic expression to make the point more vivid. What Jesus doesn't do is get lost in cultural complexity.

If we assume again that there is something here for Christians now to emulate because Jesus is Lord, and therefore example as well as Savior, then what is it? I think it is that Christians are always to ensure, as far as they can, that their arrangements for every aspect of life are low-key, direct and uncomplicated—in that sense simple.

The group of people I live with used to eat together once a week. We took turns cooking a beautiful meal for eleven people. We thought it was important to share food and time in this way. However these were not always joyful occasions. The cook often found preparation a burden (especially if there was a rush from work or there were babies to feed at the same time); the two trestle tables were awkward to erect; eleven adequate chairs took time to find—and longer to put away. Waiting until the last person came home meant tired, hungry, cross children and irritable parents.

It is different now. We eat together three times a week— one is a hospitality lunch—and mostly they are the happy occasions we have always aimed for. Why the difference? At least three people share the preparation; we have a simpler meal on a large, permanent table with two long, solid benches; evening meals are early and any latecomers have their food kept for them. The simplifying of both expectations and methods—the cultural baggage—has led to a more harmonious, gentle atmosphere.

The factors operating in this small example can be widely applied. Intention is never to be lost in organization. Purpose is never to be frustrated by what surrounds it; the end is never to be overwhelmed by the means. We are always to keep in mind our original aim—to see the wood for the trees. And what is the intention, purpose or end? In general it is to live in the kingdom of God in this world, which means both worship of the king and service for him. Within that general purpose there will be more specific tasks, according to the time of opportunity that each disciple is in.

There is still another aspect to consider. Not only are

Christian disciples to be direct, unconfused and undeterred by distractions; they are also to exhibit a certain sort of naivety. Jesus told his seventy, "I send you out as sheep in the midst of wolves".[20] (That's what Jesus himself was amongst his executioners.) There is an unsophistication, a straightforward ingenuousness given by this metaphor which is always to characterize Christians in the world. Openness has to stand among guile. Honesty has to rub shoulders with deceit. Words are to mean what they say.

These additional dimensions, here summarized as directness and openness, are part of Christian simplicity. They are interwoven with attitudes to possessions. Learning to live them becomes part of our journey in the direction of simplicity. Practical consequences are many.

For instance, businesses and other organizations where Christians carry any authority will be marked by openness among staff, lack of secretiveness over policy and a refreshing diminishing of social importance based on rank. In churches, politicking, lobbying and maneuvering will be out of place. Christian families—natural or extended—will seek between their members open honesty, monitored by love and respect and devoid of subterfuge.

Together

This "going in the direction of simplicity", as an answer to the dilemma of how to work out a simple Christian life, gains another component as soon as people begin to go in this direction *together*. Perhaps an intentional community forms. Maybe a house group begins to share consumer durables, such as a washing machine, as well as in prayer. A single person joins two parents and their children to form an extended family, using a joint house and maybe garden tools. Or a cluster of neighbors begins to share a sewing machine and freezer and the decisions about replacing these.

As soon as any of those things begins, a group consensus develops about how members of that group should live. For some groupings these steps have been the starting-point of a more communal life. For others they are signs of such a life. But whichever way it happens, here is another partial answer to questions such as "What is selfish accumulation?" and "What does *essential* mean?" By discussion, prayer, decision and practice, individuals find a concrete expression for the simple life by accepting some degree of group guidance. Without such group life, individual action and direction will waver. So strong are the pressures for greater and greater consumption, greater and greater spending, that we need others' help to stand firm. Here is a simple illustration of what I mean.

In New Zealand there is no real shortage of electricity and our family has more than enough heaters. How easy it is to press the switch in winter and enjoy the summer temperature in our living room. Everyone else does. But for the last two-and-a-half years we have shared our home with a younger couple, part of our community, who are very aware of both wasteful energy consumption and the insulation provided by woolen clothes. Their example has had its effect on us. Not that we use no electric heat, but it's not the first step. Warm vests, jerseys, tights and socks are now in our drawers and they go on before the heaters! The result is a great reduction in our power consumption and much less irritability from stuffy, hot atmospheres.

So accepted are very high levels of food consumption, energy usage and consumer goods ownership that we are very easily convinced that a luxury of yesterday is a necessity of today. One person alone, or even one family, does not have enough psychological stamina, ability or spiritual insight to stand alone as a pyramid of simplicity in a desert

of consumer waste. The New Testament gives special promi-
nence to God being with Christians gathered in his name
to seek his guidance.[21] Ronald Sider has a good expression.
He says Christians ought to be together in "communities of
loving defiance".[22]

This advocacy of community guidance is seen, by some,
as just another decline into a pharisaical subcult of conforming nonconformity such as we have already disavowed. But
while that is a danger, that is not the intention and needn't
be the reality. Encouragement rather than prescription
should be the expectation. The family which had two gifted
violinists would be encouraged to spend $1500 on each of
two instruments of merit, because that family had gifts to
be enhanced and used to bring joy to others. The family
would cut back somewhere else or the group to which the
family belonged, if it is real about its intention, would be
willing to contribute. So individuality is recognized as having its place and individual needs respected and catered for.

What is the solution then to these intellectual puzzles of
how to live simply and with Christian integrity? How do we
actualize a truly Christian lifestyle without resorting to specific prescriptions for ourselves and for those with whom we
associate? Do we have to fall back after all on a legalistic
system of rules, regulations, prohibitions and absolute ceil-
ings? Do we therefore have only generalizations?

We have a general directive—always towards simplicity,
bound to a living personal relationship with God, able to be
applied to any culture (unless below subsistence level). Are
we left to "go it alone"? God calls into being fellowships of
believers and it is these which help members make specific
decisions. Have we gone far enough towards particulars? I
think so. Go further and we will enter a religion of law, not
grace.

The church simple

The fellowship of believers deciding together through the guidance of the Holy Spirit—what is that? Why, the local church—or part of it. The local church must come back to being central in Christian faith and practice, from being a random get-together for Sunday hymn singing. It has to be concerned with questions such as "How shall we live?" because upon the answer depends what the church "will look like". And what "it looks like" is its witness. Not only will the church in its local dimension help individual members with matters of lifestyle, but the churches as institutions have also to answer that question for themselves.

Wouldn't it be marvellous if suddenly, but benignly, churches lost all their property and invested wealth? The issue of "how to live" would really be pressed then! Because the church is overall incredibly rich,[23] the change is staggering to contemplate. The church with all its material assets seems a long way from Jesus' instructions to "sell and give", "have purses which do not grow old", "do not build up treasure on earth" but "build up treasure which is in heaven".[24] But criticism of the church's real estate holdings, or suggestions that some of the regional and locally held assets should be sold and the money given to the poor, are seldom taken seriously. They are not even voiced in the places which count. Such ideas are usually pooh-poohed as being naive, unrealistic or inappropriate for the twentieth century. They are dismissed as the crazy notions of a superspiritual few. And this is rather sad. The church is more influenced by the materialistic, security-conscious but respectable world around it, than by the advocacy of its own people based on its own authority, the Scriptures. That advocacy may not always be correct, but at least it ought to be listened to.

There are in fact many Christian groups, projects and

communities sharing help and decision-making at all levels —though, by comparison with the individualistic pattern of life endemic in our society, they are still relatively uncommon. One of the tragedies of our age is that so few of these are parish churches in the full sense of the term in any of the historic denominations. Most which work as real extended households lie outside the mainline denominational structure and have become churches themselves either by declaration or default.[25]

Somehow the church "militant here on earth" seems out of step with the commands of Jesus it supposedly proclaims. The incongruity strikes many outside the church, even though they may live richly themselves, but it is not seen by those of us inside. The reason is clear enough. In our private and family lives we have taken on board the consumer society and its values and so, when we assemble as "church", we exhibit the same traits. The kingdom of Christ has become, in lifestyle, the kingdom of this world.

There is a great need to get ourselves out of a mind-set that dismisses the advocates of simplicity as naive or way-out. To any disciple the commands of Jesus ought to be as pertinent as contemporary secular materialism and the scientific and technological processes on which that way is based. We unquestioningly accept the latter as "facts of life". Why don't we do the same with the teaching of the Lord we love and serve? If naivety seems the problem, we could argue that the church is naive to think it can be a good witness to a selfless gospel which it then denies—by absorbing many of the values of a consumer society, based on selfish greed.

The church will, of course, never undergo a benign property confiscation. Confiscation, if ever it occurred, would be accompanied by other deprivations, if not persecution. The church needs to undertake its own radical revolution. Wouldn't it be tremendous to see councils, synods, circuits, conferences, presbyteries, vestries and all the rest really opening themselves to the question, "How should the church live?"

No one is asking for a replacement of every church hall with a tent or every manse with a trailer. But I wish we would all ponder how far the church has departed from God's will in owning revenue-producing office blocks and great slabs of expensive housing land, and investing in trade, industry and even extra land and premises held against a rainy day. The net result is to make a mockery of Jesus' ethic to have less, not more—to live more simply and less lavishly.

That the church is to dispense material help is clear. In Acts, that exciting chronicle of early church life, people brought wealth and laid it at the apostles' feet.[26] So the church has a good historical precedent in having organizations and agencies which "give to the poor". And Paul gave a good deal of time to collecting from some churches for the Christians in Jerusalem.[27] But that is no justification for turning the church into a business house or giant landowner on the tenuous grounds that such investment is a good hedge against inflation, sound security for nervous bankers or a backstop for declining donations. The widow with her cruse of oil, constantly refilled as its supplies were diminished, should be the financial model for the community of faith, not the merchant with his bigger and better barns.[28]

The church and wealth

Consequences of the church's identification with material wealth are far-reaching. One is for the predominantly middle-class population of many churches, which close themselves to others by their members social attributes of speech, dress and activity. A man I know from a factory floor tried to go to one such church, but said to me afterwards, "I just didn't feel right with those people. They're different!" He was referring to more than their comely speech and demure manner or the "offense of the gospel".

Another consequence is inflexible church structures and strategy, unready to change or meet changing situations because buildings and other property take on their own life-force. "We can't do that because we'd lose too much on the property if we sold it", or "That was built by the church years ago—we can't change that!" The material investment in these cases is so important that it dictates all. The wealth of the church is not the only reason for its inflexibility (sometimes struggling churches also are made inflexible by their being excessively poor), but it is a significant one.

A third consequence is illustrated by this story:

> One day a rich but miserly chassid came to a rabbi. The rabbi led him to a window.
> "Look out there", he said, "and tell me what you see".
> "People", answered the rich man.
> Then the rabbi led him to a mirror. "What do you see now?" he asked.
> "I see myself", answered the chassid.
> Then the rabbi said, "Behold, in the window there is glass and in the mirror there is glass. But the glass in the mirror is covered with a little silver, and no sooner is a little silver added than you cease to see others and see only yourself."

Dependence on money and pride in physical property makes poor, not rich, the congregation that trusts in these. The church most financially privileged in the New Testament was also the one most poverty-stricken spiritually.[29] The two need not, but often do, go together.

Many alternative possibilities

A church, whose members follow out their discipleship in the direction of simplicity, has open to it adventurous possibilities. For example, it could be a wonderful place for young married couples beginning to have families. One group of "the poor" in Western society is the overspent, overwrought young marrieds. Their apartments are soon full of furniture and appliances; they are rich—but they are poor. They work furiously to find enough money to maintain and increase their standard of living. They need rescuing from the prison of material agglomeration, by being shown simpler, happier ways and by being given practical help to get what they need to live as creative Christians in a world of colossal expense. Long before lifestyle literature became fashionable, Jacques Ellul wrote, as he talked about the presence of the kingdom of God in the modern world:

> *So long as the solidarity between Christians is not expressed in mutual help which will permit everyone to find a balanced life, to discover a style of life which truly expresses his faith (and not in order to avoid starving), it will be only a matter of words.*[30]

That means giving and lending each other money—great chunks of it if necessary—rooms, apartments and anything else. "Sell and give!"

Boat people and political refugees, the dispossessed from many nations—they are "the poor" too. Churches or groups of churches can pressure their governments to allow immigration, and they can offer a house or rent-free apartment and long-term compassionate, dignified and warm friendship over several years as the newcomers adapt several hundred years of culture in a few short months. How dare we stay rich while others starve, or live in luxury while others have no shelter.

Other church members, moving in the direction of simplicity and thus having money, time and possessions available for others, may offer a self-contained part of their house, or a room, to a solo parent or an adolescent in need of a home. Either of these people may be in need of love which includes both care and financial help. A Christian commentator on the Australian scene said he thought there was tremendous need for families to live in such a way that they could invite permanently into their homes an "adopted Granny"—an older lady otherwise sent to an old persons' home, who would live as part of the family while contributing to the family life and the keeping of the house.[31]

These suggestions are neither definitive nor exhaustive, but they are practicable. I know instances where all of them work. Yet overall how many churches function like that? It's the outstanding exceptions that get noticed because the average performance is so very different. Silver needs to be removed from the glass panes in our homes and churches to transform them from mirrors of our own comfort into windows to the world.

If we have any doubts about where our responsibilities lie, perhaps the First Letter of John will dispel them:

> By this we know love, that he [Jesus Christ] laid down his life for us; and we ought to lay down our lives for the brethren. But if anyone has the world's goods and sees his brother in need, yet closes his heart against him, how does God's love abide in him? Little children, let us not love in word or speech but in deed and in truth. [32]

Nonrenewable resources

We cannot discuss Christian simplicity without touching on

the debate about nonrenewable resources, because world shortages of key natural resources thrust it on us. Christians who become convinced that they must go in the direction of simplicity will find themselves using less oil, metal and similar materials. Indeed Christians of this ilk often stand very close, in their attitude to the created world, to that adopted by ecology action groups for whom "nonrenewable resources" has become a convenient catchword and slogan. Some Christians may be in such groups. That's hardly surprising because Christians have a mandate to "till and keep" the earth.[33] Use and consumption is permitted, but preservation is part of the same mandate. Also included is the teaching of Jesus we have been studying and a lot of Old Testament instruction about provision but not hoarding, such as the Exodus instruction to gather wilderness food daily but not to keep it.[34]

But Christians by and large have been thoughtless over the past fifty years about the rape of the natural world. We have been mesmerized by our relative comfort and plenty into accepting what we should have protested about. We have participated in economics built on cheap fossil fuels, leading to gas-guzzling automobiles and the development of huge petro-chemical plants producing tons of plastic—a lot of which is used for trivial purposes before being thrown away. Like the rest of the population, we have complacently accepted one product of technical advance after another without question. Why?

To answer that, consider for a moment a wider issue—an issue important for the rest of this chapter and indeed for the whole book. Harry Blamires, in his book *The Christian Mind*, wrote in 1963:

> *There is no longer a Christian mind . . . As a thinking being, the modern Christian has succumbed to*

> *secularization. He accepts religion—its morality, its worship, its spiritual culture—but he rejects the religious view of life, the view which sets all earthly issues within the context of the eternal, the view which relates all human problems—social and political, cultural—to the doctrinal foundation of the Christian faith, the view which sees all things here below in terms of God's supremacy and earth's transitoriness in terms of heaven and hell.* [35]

Again he said:

> *Except over a very narrow field of thinking, chiefly touching questions of strictly personal conduct, we Christians in the modern world accept, for the purpose of mental activity, a frame of reference constructed by the secular mind and a set of criteria reflecting secular evaluations. There is no Christian mind; there is no shared field of discourse in which we can move at ease as thinking Christians by trodden ways and past established landmarks.* [36]

There is of course a Christian *theology*—indeed not one, but many. Theologians know how to talk to each other, but that's not what is meant here. What lacks and lags is thought and thinkers from a specifically Christian starting-point, about all aspects of the world in which we live.

John Taylor, the author of another very popular Christian analysis of affluence, tackles the same problem this way:

> *We need to study the Bible text, preferably in groups, until we have made its basic frame of reference our own and can instinctively apply it to our contemporary situation. We should try to become as naturally at home in this God-centered and world-embracing way of looking at things as a good Marxist in his*

quite different ideology. Only so can we guard the freedom of our mind against the insidious pressures that are being brought to bear upon it from all sides. [37]

Wise comment, but often we limit biblical discussion and application to individual morals or pietistic insights, or dismiss it as irrelevant altogether.

Now consider what happens when someone in a private conversation, a board meeting, a gathering of church leaders or a Bible study group begins "to apply instinctively" the Bible's basic frame of reference to affluence and such issues as nonrenewable resources. Moved by tenets such as "Love your neighbor" and "Till and keep", such a person might begin wondering about oil-fired central heating, suggesting (in New Zealand at least) that it be replaced by using hydroelectric power. Further, he might suggest, that heating a whole house or a whole church plant is an unnecessary luxury anyway. Or if industry is the topic, the same person might argue that the beautiful new plastic wrapping and printing factory should change to paper wrapping—to use renewable forestry and prevent blowing into the atmosphere every twelve minutes the factory's plastic dust-laden air, to cut down the nonbiodegradable waste left at every picnic place and to conserve petro-chemical supplies. Moreover he might well ask that lots of excessive packaging and over-wrapping cease altogether.

Many times I have noticed that if such a proponent raises these issues, we are likely to look down, shuffle our feet, then embarrassed, puzzled, incredulous, angry or even patronizing, dismiss the question by hurrying to the next topic. We are not used to people thinking like that. On the other hand the questioner will feel out of place. It's obvious he has raised an issue with which the others cannot cope. The likelihood is that he will either stop thinking that way or find a few people somewhere else with whom he can reinforce his prejudices. The problem is not that people disagree with him, but that no dialogue is entered into because the thought tracks aren't there. Blamires' diagnosis is thus frequently quite correct—there is no Christian mind. And it's worth noting, as an interesting sidelight, that such a questioner will often be made more welcome by humanists and other variously motivated environmentalists who sympathize with his concerns.

We have to face situations as they really are. Although some Christians have said "No" to things the way they are and have tried to inject alternative ideas, most Christians as individuals and churches have gone along with the tide. Every householder who uses plastic bags, every shareholder who gains dividends from petro-chemical or fertilizer industries, is encouraging the working out of a secular world view based upon exploitive consumption. Such an outlook contains within itself the seeds of its own destruction, because the resources on which it feeds will not last forever.

There is an urgent need therefore for Christians to think out of a biblical framework, to apply themselves in thought and action to such questions as: "What will we do about nonrenewable resources?" A biblical world view, integrated with all the professional expertise that can be mustered, needs to be put together by Christians who, wherever they are, can authenticate their contentions with living demonstrations of alternative ways.

Celebration and joy

What disaster if Christian simplicity is seen as a series of austere and gloomy prohibitions. I've tried to guard against that by insisting that the simple life is not a legalistic creed but a God-linked, communally agreed direction. However, there is another facet. The Christian life is expected by biblical writers to be alive with joy.

Christ himself is appointed, according to one of the great Messianic passages in Isaiah, to bring garlands, oil of gladness and other symbols of joy.[38] Because of the liberty and forgiveness Jesus brings, other New Testament writers like Paul enjoin Christian believers to rejoice in the Lord. And according to Luke, joy was in fact an overwhelming characteristic of the original disciples after Jesus had risen from the dead and of new believers like the man who, with his household, believed and was baptized.

So much does joy lie at the centre of the faith-life experienced by Christians of the early church that it was seen as one of the signs of the presence of the Holy Spirit.[39] A glance at any topical concordance reveals that joy is a widely dispersed biblical idea, especially in the New Testament.

All of this does not mean that Christians then were, or Christians now are, to live in a state of continuous intoxication, smiling, back-slapping or using a contrived "hallelujah" vocabulary. That should be seen for what it is—a pretence or, at best, a learned cultic response. Affliction, suffering and trials of various sorts form part of the life of humanity which Christians share. But this deep joy in Christ is present even in such bad times. Joy belongs to the kingdom of God, and that kingdom is partially yet actually present now. Joy therefore can be expected to be present too, though sometimes hindered by sin and sorrow.

Although not artificial nor dependent on circumstances, joy is still to be passionate. If Christians follow the biblical pattern, they will find themselves caught up in various emotional and communal expressions of joy. For instance the Christians at Ephesus were encouraged to "address one another in psalms, hymns and spiritual songs", making "melody to the Lord".[40] Giving expression to this joy is an important part of the simple life to which Jesus calls us. Part of that expression is a deep certainty and unshakeable conviction that God is God and we need not be anxious. "Have no fear, little flock." "Put away anxious thoughts", says Jesus in verses 32 and 22 of Luke 12.

Another aspect of joy to be reawakened is our understanding of Christian celebration. William Booth, founding hero of the Salvation Army, is often quoted as saying of music, "Why should the devil have all the best tunes?" We might likewise ask, "Why should we have all the best *parties?*" Especially "why?" at times like Christmas, which are still tokenly Christian celebrations but which have been bastardized by commercial interests, and often stereotyped or formalized out of all joy by the church. After all, what a birthday! God breaking through in a new way to man's condition! God himself becoming incarnate in human form! No wonder the early Christians took over an old pagan festival in order to celebrate such a birth. And as it was a birth which led to an atoning death, so awe as well as joy was an appropriate ingredient of the celebration.

For ages, Christmas has been for me an agony—a bitter realization that, with the pressure of Christmas the way it is, Christmas the way I thought it should be was nearly impossible. But last Christmas, in the presence of the people in my church with whom I live communally, I felt closer to the sort of celebration that seemed appropriate than ever before.

The day began early, with children in the families opening traditional Christmas stockings containing a few simple gifts —a perfectly ordinary part of the cultural heritage.

Then at 8 a.m. our community, which then only numbered eleven people, joined the local church congregation for celebration of the Lord's Supper in a traditional way.

After that the community, plus house guests, had breakfast of various homemade bread rolls served with coffee.

Then everyone moved to another room, dressed up as Mary, Joseph, the Wise Men and all the other characters and took part in a tableau mime to a narration read from Scripture. Carols were also sung. All took part—visitors, children, adults. There were no spectators.

The last of the Wise Men presented to the Christ-child an envelope of money, given in anonymous but sacrificial amounts by the community members. This was later sent to a Christian agency for use in an area where aid was desperately needed.

When the pageant was finished presents, often handmade, were exchanged as a reminder to each other that Christ came into the world for us all, and then the celebration concluded, three hours after it had begun, with a dance of thanksgiving. Later one community family shared Christmas dinner with their relatives, while the rest of us invited to our meal a person who otherwise would have had no celebration at all.

Everyone who took part felt strangely moved. The breakfast was simple but special. What could have been "dressing up with the kids" became a rich entry into the Mary and Joseph story.[41] In giving substantially (not just symbolically) to those in need through an agency we could trust, we felt we had acted in accordance with the message of the Judgment story in Matthew 25—that giving to the poor is giving to Christ himself.[42] After all, Christmas is his birthday.

We have already noticed the danger of letting an example become a model and ultimately a rule. I therefore share this experience apologetically. The only intention is to spur others to create new forms of Christian celebration which are appropriate to both the event celebrated and the culture in which the celebration takes place. Prayer, thought, imagination and preparation is required, based on a determination not to allow the significance to be undermined by current practice.

And we need not stop at Christmas, or even other church festivals such as Easter Day and Pentecost. Birthdays celebrate the coming into the world of unique individuals, each entrusted with gifts and abilities to make a contribution to the life of the church and society. And they are worth celebrating—madly!

Food, drink, songs and a prayer of dedication for the year ahead help us to make a fuss of that person in a wholehearted recognition of his or her worth. Not a party that gives the hero a hangover for days—how does that help?—but one which encourages the person to be the child of God that he or she can be.

And in the life of any individual, family, group or church there will be farewells, returns, thank-yous, recoveries and lives reunited with God after repentance, all of which allow great room for initiative, spontaneity and creativity in celebration. Celebration can be a very frequent and important part of life. Not only are the celebrations joyous occasions when the deep-seated joy of the Christian faith has opportunity to sparkle to the surface, but they are symbolic of the foundational security, truth and assurance which being in the kingdom provides.

In living in this way, we are following through the Judaistic tradition that Christ came to fulfil, which put a great emphasis on the festivals celebrating what God had done for his chosen people. For instance, by remembering at the Passover God's rescue of them from Egypt, the people of Israel received assurance of his leading in the future. As we celebrate, we do something very similar.

Christians are to be a simple, celebrating people. Their "parties" are not to be empty rituals or stereotyped formal services. They will be alive, virile, probably noisy and crackling with joy. If they are not, we might well ask some probing questions about the reality of the life with God which the participants profess. Joy is one sure sign of gospel simplicity —a simplicity always to be lived by the people of God.

3
Privacy

Conformity to privacy is as much a curse as conformity to affluence. The two stand hand in hand. Affluence is the profusion of wealth, seen especially in the accumulation of consumer goods by oneself or one's family. Privacy is the concentration upon self and upon those who belong to me intimately. It is reflected in the attitude which says:

> "I don't want to be involved—I don't want to put myself at risk. I just want to live as I want to and I acknowledge your right to do the same."

High salaries and high fences go together. Christians as much as other people in the community want private gardens, individual houses or apartments, their own cars, a bedroom each, portable television sets bringing standardized but individually controlled entertainment to living rooms, separate newspapers, individual heat sources, personal credit cards . . . and many other similar things. The more affluent the person, the more private the lifestyle. In India, a traveller on a crowded train can be private by turning his back while he says his prayers. Here, we seem to need at least a room. Affluence allows us a wealthy privacy that is denied to most people in the world.

It is important that we question this path we are taking. Is it not true that more and more privacy only isolates us more and more? The loneliness of a student in a single room in a big dorm is now clearly recognized[1]—a loneliness from which some personalities never recover. The "housewife syndrome" or anxiety neurosis common to many married women in the suburbs is also acknowledged.[2] By extension, could it be that one of the causes of the banal, superficial fellowship experienced in many of our churches is the isolation cult induced by the privacy we so easily accept as an inalienable right? If and when we do try to live, even for a week or two, more communally or in an "open house", we find it a terrible strain and with relief turn again to our cozy cocoon. Our affluent tradition has molded us. So private are we that even moderate exposure to each other is exhausting.

Privacy today often goes beyond the search for living or personal privacy. It has colored our whole attitude to life and created an outlook of easy tolerance and lethargic apathy. In recent years this has even pervaded the once radical, socially involved world of youth. A *Time* magazine feature stated in November 1977:

> . . . *what clearly emerges among the vast majority of European youth is a profound and perhaps worrisome distaste for all forms of politics. The danger is that this attitude reflects a growing indifference about almost everything. That is an awful possibility.*[3]

Moreover the young are not the only part of society possessed by this spirit. So widespread is this characteristic that it is easily and unknowingly inbibed by many Christians, whose blatant lack of involvement in the problems of our society is a denial of the incarnation itself.

Worst of all, continued privacy seeking culminates in lack of justice. Matters which ought to be challenged are, because of private indolence, not bothered about and injustice is allowed to go unchecked. Examples of this range from minor social problems such as littering, vandalism or bullying in public places to major head-in-the-sand attitudes regarding race disputes in local suburbs, the fate of political prisoners under right- and left-wing regimes or the predicament of exploited workers in developing countries. But passive disinterest on an international scale takes root at home and so the minor, homegrown incidents are those which should first and continually attract our attention and Christian response.

The move to greater and greater privacy is not the only significant trend in our society but, because of its extent and pervasiveness, some commentators are predicting the collapse in the West of community relationships as we have known them.[4] That collapse has been under way for some time and shows little sign of reversal. The tragedy is that those who are Christians in such a world are unthinkingly contributing to its demise.

Prayer, privacy and people

What is Christian attitude to privacy? There is no better staring point than to begin with Jesus and his relationship to prayer, privacy and people.

Jesus followed the rabbinic tradition of talking, eating and living with his closest disciples. They went with him to celebrations[5] and to dinners in people's homes.[6] They listened while he further explained to them the truth he was trying to teach others.[7] They worked with him, and he commended them when they did right and corrected them when they did wrong.[8] Sometimes they withdrew to be private—to pray together[9] or to relax.

Once in India I talked with a young man who was learning the sitar. For three years he had lived in the constant company of his master. He shared his house and went with him to concerts and festivals, watching, listening, absorbing, then practicing under his direction. He was taught the importance of music in his master's life. In the modern West we don't easily understand the force of that sort of learning experience, but it is this kind of intensive, cheek-by-jowl existence that Jesus lived with his closest disciples.

But even though Jesus lived in close relationship with a chosen band, many times he wanted to be quite alone. The Gospels record him going up a mountain, into a wilderness or to the room of a house.[10] Each of his isolation times was either before a crucial decision (e.g., choosing the apostles)[11] or after an exhausting ministry (e.g., teaching and feeding the five thousand).[12] Presumably there were unrecorded times too, but the instances we do know about indicate a moving into privacy followed, or preceded by, a moving *out*—into contact with others, whether a huge crowd, his disciples, the apostles, some individual needing help or some antagonist firing questions. The ministry was public; the preparation and aftermath were private.

The privacy of Jesus was "with God" privacy. To say from the recorded teaching and examples of Jesus that we therefore have a timeless principle or pattern of prayerful privacy may be too strong. The words "principle" and "pattern" have connotations of recipe and rigidity which the texts do not support. We can point though to a rhythm—a varied one maybe, but nevertheless a rhythm—mixing public ministry and private communion. This rhythm is caused by life's events and yet also influences them. It contains a flexible withdrawal for prayer as a complementary part of a life spent with people. No profile of Jesus is properly drawn unless these twin aspects are clearly outlined. And the profile is still erroneous unless the outward is seen to depend upon the inward. Prime time is spent intimately with God the Father.

This practice of private prayer is reinforced by Jesus' specific teaching in the Sermon on the Mount:

> When you pray, go into your own room, shut your door and pray to your Father privately. Your Father who sees all private things will reward you. [13]

Whatever the cultural details (whether this was an individual's room or a small grain-and-produce store in the house) or even if the verse is interpreted allegorically to mean praying in one's own mind and heart,[14] the main thrust is clear enough. In contrast to the flamboyancy of the hypocrites, Jesus' disciples are to put themselves alone with God. The reward is private or secret too. It comes as inner fortitude, peace and enrichment to equip oneself for the next task, as in Jesus' pre-crucifixion experience when three times during the night he prayed privately while the apostles slept.[15]

"With God" privacy is the downbeat of the rhythm of Jesus' life. The *upbeat* is community togetherness and the public ministry extending from it. This idea of togetherness, community or fellowship is common in Scripture. It has its roots in the Old Testament idea of a tribe and a chosen people.[16] Paul develops it in the New Testament as one aspect of the doctrine of the church and it is this idea which we now examine.

The communal shape of the church

Fellowship is expressed by the use of words derived from the Greek verb *koinoneo*, which means "to give a share in something to someone". So the noun *koinonia* means "sharing, having or giving a share, fellowship". And what we have a share in, when we use *koinonia* in a specifically Christian sense, is God. We have fellowship in Christ,[17] we have fellowship in the Holy Spirit[18] and we have fellowship with the

Father.[19]

Fellowship in God then, because it is experienced by all who follow Jesus into the kingdom, links Christians together. Bruce Milne puts it accurately:

> *Paul sets out the teaching on fellowship in his letters. In each of them the call to live in fellowship with one another follows upon an exposition of the basis of fellowship, our common union with Christ in death and resurrection. Thus Romans 12:3–13 is preceded by Romans 6:1ff, Galatians 6:1–5 is preceded by 2:20; Ephesians 4:7ff is preceded by 2:5–6; Colossians 3:8–17 is preceded by 2:12f and 3.1f. The call to live in fellowship is then a joyous, happy call. It is a call to make real in our Christian relationships that which God has already given us.* [20]

The corporate base is also expressed in the notion of togetherness. This concept is implied not only when the apostle talks about fellowship itself, but also when he describes what it is we share—whether gifts, goods, money, functions, suffering, hospitality, affection, burden-bearing, restoration, unity, equality, Christ's peace, worship and thanksgiving.[21]

At the heart of all this Pauline teaching is love, the supreme quality flowing from Jesus' new commandment to "love one another as I have loved you",[22] a commandment given to the disciples immediately after the footwashing at the Last Supper and immediately before the crucifixion. This communal, sacrificial, love-for-each-other side of Jesus' call was not always perceived. I wonder if the rich young ruler realized for instance that, when Jesus invited him to give up all he had and follow him,[23] Jesus was standing amongst his disciples. The call to follow was a call to give up "the world", yes, but also a call to join a band, a tribe, a gathering, a people and indeed a kingdom within which love was to be shown beyond conventional limits.

Paul really understood that dimension of Christian discipleship. Theologically the local church as he described it was an assembly of called ones,[24] intended to epitomize in its corporate life all that Jesus taught and did and all that the New Testament writers instructed. It was a fellowship of the forgiven and a company of caring people within which, if the great metaphors of the church (such as the body of Christ[25]) are understood, every Christian was to have a place, a right, a function and a contribution. And it was a fellowship that reaches out in caring forgiveness to all who need it. That is an essential vision of which churches need to be frequently reminded today. Finding the words and verses is easy—one only needs a concordance. The challenge comes in finding the deeds. For this one needs a lifetime!

"With God" privacy today

To try to develop in one's own life these twin characteristics of "with God" *privacy* and outgoing *involvement* with others is to experience conflict sooner or later with generally accepted patterns of living. The clash comes first when a person tries to be alone with God. Although privacy is one powerful trend in Western societies, there are other powerful influences stridently demanding admission into our lives. Sound comes at the flick of one switch, visual invasion at the click of another, while the telephone intrudes at any time day or night. Then mobility of one sort or another brings many visitors to the door. When added to other responsibilities, all this leads to constant activism which relentlessly squeezes our time with God.

Yet in terms of our reflection on time in chapter 1, there is a "time for prayer". If the example and teaching of Jesus

are at all compelling—and they will be if we are Christians—
effective living for and with others will demand time spent
with God. A rule for praying, say daily at 6 a.m., is not
implied, but time alone with God as refreshment or preparation certainly is. Minutes, hours, even days with God—on
the beach, in the park, at one's desk or in bed—to read,
ponder, talk, listen, cry, laugh and sing with God are vital.

Urging this kind of privacy must not be seen as supporting
the trend to more and more attitudinal and sociological
privacy. Indeed dynamic effort is needed to break out of the
typical self-centered, comfort-filled, consumer-goods-ori-
ented privacy into time with God. More about this later.[26]
Enough to note here that the life of a Christian disciple is
scarcely thinkable without time—great slashes of it—spent
specifically in God's presence.

Difficulties

Further difficulties and clashes come when we try to apply
to our contemporary life either the community togetherness
emphasized by Paul or the master/disciple relationship
adopted by Jesus and his earliest followers. Take the example of Jonathan.

He had gone into hospital for surgery, but he had hidden
the fact from fellow church members. His wife and family
had made their own arrangements. They coped alone. Why?
They shouldn't be concerned. All this he told me at a conference where the speaker had talked about the doctrine of the
church. The studies had been based on Paul's letter to the
Ephesians, so people's attention had been drawn to the
household of God, united in Jesus Christ which "grows into
a holy temple in the Lord", the *gifts* of the Spirit "for the
equipment of the saints, the work of ministry, the building
up of the body of Christ" and the *body*, "joined and knit

together", each part "working properly . . . and upbuilding itself in love".[27]

The speaker had explained that all this implied mutual responsibility within a congregation in caring for, provoking, encouraging and loving each other while growing together in God's will. He had tried to be practical by talking about visiting each other and sharing needs, sadnesses and joys. Jonathan was provoked to say that, while he saw clearly both the biblical base and practical desirability for what the speaker said, his own experience over many years of church life was very different. He acknowledged that he and many others had moved from the biblical model, but he didn't know what to do about it. And this was a warm, amiable, biblically informed and respected Christian leader. He is typical of thousands.

And it is a real problem. All of us share with Jonathan, to a lesser or greater degree, the forces which press him. Our increasingly private way of life, which affluence, technical means and the last vestiges of Victorian propriety have thrust upon us is antithetical to any real, down-to-earth expression of Christian fellowship. It makes real talking and listening hard, corporate prayer less frequent, and appropriate, concerned caring for each other distant. We are so *isolated*. We have everything we need—or so we think—inside the four-walled shell in which we dwell. We hardly have to depend on each other at all! With food in the freezer and gas in the tank, we think we can be self-sufficient. We like to have at least one of everything we occasionally use in case we run out—and preferably another for spare in case the first one breaks!

The physical privacy in which we live hinders us from the emotional and spiritual interdependence offered by genuine fellowship and suffering, burden-bearing and all the rest which the New Testament writers urge. Great effort has to be expended to reach each other before we can even begin to talk (not many of us are just over the back fence). And the likelihood is that my friend will be watching his favorite TV program, playing squash or attending one of the myriad committee meetings which the church holds. The telephone is often the saving technological grace, but it lacks the dimensions of sight, smell and touch which are so important when we meet together. It inhibits intimacy. It certainly can be a great savior but, if we didn't have it, perhaps we would live more closely. We cannot escape the conclusion that there are dominant ingredients in the very way we live that are opposed to Christian communal interdependence.

We can rejoice that there has been since the 1950s, and especially in the 1960s and 1970s, a worldwide recovery of fellowship in the church. Small groups of one sort or another are increasingly commonplace across nearly every denomination in nearly every country. They vary in character and purpose, but most have fellowship somewhere in their intention. Bruce Milne, already quoted, calls fellowship an idea "whose hour has come".[28]

Though this may give us some reason for satisfaction, much of this worldwide trend falls short of implementing in our day the caring, sharing congregation which we have seen to be biblical. Even when people meet weekly in a group, the amount of real contact and care is limited. If we are serious about obeying the biblical pattern, we have to find ways to come closer together and to be more frequently in touch. That will not automatically guarantee greater love and care, but it will help facilitate it. So for churches, especially in town and cities, what other communal alternatives are available?

Some practical alternatives

Possible moves away from privacy are excitingly varied. We could have in any local church, additional to the already developing weekly groups, one or more of the following:

(a) *Extended families*, i.e., nuclear families with one or two extra people living permanently in them;

(b) *Neighborhood worship clusters*, i.e., two or three family units in one street or an apartment complex worshipping together, say once or twice a week, in addition to Sunday worship;

(c) *Regions of care*, i.e., the local church informally and easily divided into areas of care, led by people with pastoral gifts;

(d) *Intentional communities*, i.e., people deliberately moving to live in adjoining houses or apartments, from which there are many possibilities in extending togetherness;

(e) *Mission groups*, i.e., Christians gathering in groups around various tasks and services.

There can be various combinations of some or all of these —this list does not exhaust the possibilities. It is worth exploring more deeply what happens when such moves are implemented. Let's consider just two from this list of alternatives.

Further exploration:
neighborhood worship clusters

Take neighborhood worship clusters. As soon as three or four living units try to get together regularly, the question of "when" arises. One time after another is found to be difficult or impossible. Therefore people have to change. Perhaps one person, taking a turn, has to look after all the children. Or the worship has to be designed to cater for children, which means a lot of special preparation. If it means household units taking turns to look after the pre-school children, that leads to adults getting to know those children better, then becoming familiar with each others' houses. Or perhaps a working man will try and rearrange his starting time with his boss. He is taking one small step towards shaping his style of living, starting from the things that he considers most important. Or a mother will change her children's eating times. Again she is becoming less private by allowing other influences to determine habits even if, at the beginning, they cause considerable unrest.

Is all this just unimportant practical trivia, unrelated to spiritual purpose? Life is the sum total of trivia. There are very few large, important things. Events, happenings and experiences are usually the joining of lots of little arrangements. They are *worth* discussing. Failure to do so often leads to the defeat of idealism. If we are serious about living in the kingdom, then every part of life is to be brought within that intention.

If such a worship cluster persists, a number of consequences will follow. At times the worship will be boring, repetitious or self-centered. That will demand a rethink of what is worship and a request for help from those who have insight into, or responsibility for, worship in the congregation. Some individuals will annoy others and therefore there will need to grow acceptance on the part of some and character change on the part of others. Because the worship will include prayer for each other, an understanding of each others' lives will develop. Friendship might come, too. Intentional community could ultimately arise.

In practice the scenario may not read as easily or as fruitfully as this, but certainly there will be some invasion of personal privacy by caring, community life. Some church members may not like the invasion, but at least they, too, will have to think about themselves in relation to others. And there is always encouragement. C. S. Lewis wrote:

> *The sacrifice of selfish privacy which is daily demanded of us is daily repaid one hundredfold in the true growth of personality which the life of the body encourages.* [29]

Further exploration: intentional communities

"Intentional community" of a Christian character is a topic on its own about which a considerable literature has lately grown.[30] "Intentional" indicates that such communities come together by deliberate decision, not by historical, familial or tribal evolution. The name may stand for a group of hundreds living in many extended households, or for a dozen or fewer people living together in various degrees of communal involvement. The "shape" can be colorfully varied. One group I know built four small houses on four corners of a block of land, with communal space in the middle. Another group-growing-into-community (in which I live) has several adjacent older houses, of which the biggest is the communal center. At present we meet formally five times a week and informally, in twos or threes across the group, many more times. A community can be urban or rural and live in separate houses, separate apartments or one large building. The degree of "togetherness" can be large or small, and can change as God guides.

Development of intentional communities, as *part* of the local church, is within the scope of any group of people who are convinced that God is calling them to let the corporate implications of their faith be seen in their pattern of life. There will be difficulties but, if they and others who lead their church decide that God is leading them that way, then through the power of the Holy Spirit sustaining their determination they will be able to meet the difficulties one by one. The possibilities in community are immense for realizing greater fellowship of a biblical nature. Imaginative worship together, corporate decision-making, admonition, encouragement, sharing of resources and possessions, offering long- or short-term hospitality without overburdening any individual, supporting each other in individual ministry, participating in the daily ups and downs of life and developing an easy openness and caring—all these possibilities are waiting to be shaped as clay waits to be thrown by a potter.

Some communities develop tasks such as printing a magazine,[31] recycling discarded commodities[32] or giving hospitality[33] to the needy. Others live together while some of their members continue working at "ordinary" employment.[34] However varied they may be, all such Christian communities share the aim of trying to work out "on the ground" the theological reality the Scriptures talk about in portraying the Christian church as a mutually loving, caring fellowship.

One of the main hindrances to the further development of community living within the church is that many of us see community as something odd, something for "the funny people", for "the radicals"—for the "beards, beads and sandals" brigade. Odd, sometimes immoral behavior ending in tragedy or a new sect often scares us from considering seriously this alternative way of living. We mustn't let it do so. It may be important to know that since apostolic times, represented in Acts chapters 2 and 4, there has been a communal streak within the church. It has always managed to exist although often seriously conditioned, not only by cultural and political factors, but by the attitude of the ruling ecclesiastical hierarchy who usually have not liked it.

Various monastic orders, such as the Franciscans of the early and later Middle Ages, and various Protestant communities which were part of the so-called "radical Reformation" kept the idea alive. The Moravians, who became one of the most prolific missionary communities ever known, continued this radical tradition and passed it on to people like John and Charles Wesley and other early Methodists. It emerged a little in various parts of the nineteenth century missionary movement and, since World War II, has grown in many parts of the world.[35]

The sheer unwillingness to change deters us too. Whatever our habits, we become set in them and they, not our spiritual ideals, determine what we do. The standards around us, especially the general expectation for independent, private living, bolster that reluctance. We are often unwilling to let the Christian truth about not counting our possessions dear, sharing suffering and loving our neighbors push us beyond the limits set by conventional society.

Families in community

When intentional community is discussed, one of the questions constantly raised is "What about the family?" The family is cracking up in our societies. It is therefore understandable that there should be concern about yet more possible stress. Christians, in addition, see the family as God-ordained and wish it to remain a strong social fabric.

If already existing families move towards such communal alternatives, especially intentional community, there is bound to be some strain caused by change, even if the change is totally satisfactory. Moving into an existing community, or beginning one after many years of individualistic or nuclear family life, is a very special task, different from continuing to live in such a community. It compares with moving one's family to another culture. We must prepare for this step and time and effort have then to be given, in the three or four years following, to learning how to *live* in the new way. But if the move is gradual, if peer group communities (where everyone has the same hassle at the same time) are avoided, the strain of beginning can be overcome. Children learn to relate to other adults, measuring their growth against them as well as their parents. That's good. They learn to mix, too, with a wider group of children of different ages, as they would have done one hundred years ago in a large family. They see, more than they did before, that their parents put high value on people and worship—provided their parents do in fact!

But a tendency of beginning groups is to try to do far too much at once: physical alteration of the property, new housing arrangements, inter-communal meetings, hospitality, and all the sacrifice and service towards which strong idealism pushes. That won't work—exhaustion results. There is a "time for community establishment" and it must be given the hours and days it needs.[36] A similar tendency is for established groups to expect new members to adjust too quickly. "Apprenticeship" allowance has to be made. And part of both of these situations is to ensure that families can live within community in such a way that husbands love their wives, wives respect their husbands, children obey their parents and fathers do not provoke their children to anger.[37]

All of this means that solid thought has to be given to achieving sufficient separation to allow the family to function as such, while shedding some of its excessive nuclear independence. For instance, husbands can't love wives who are always attending to something else. Or again, husbands will provoke their children to anger if they don't spend enough time with them. It is useless to prescribe here or anywhere else a recipe on how to live "separately together". Each situation has its own requirement, its own balance. But to the question "What about the family?" we can quite firmly say that, provided the family is given the practical importance accorded to it in Christian teaching—but not more than that—the awkwardness of change can be survived, even conquered. Moreover once that has happened, family life can flourish in community because the family is not having to carry upon its own shoulders more than absolutely necessary—the isolation of the nuclear family is avoided.

The communal or communitarian alternatives all stem from the ideas of fellowship outlined by Paul in his epistles or from Luke, particularly in the early part of Acts. But there is also application stemming from the master/disciple relationship which we saw exhibited by Jesus and his apostles. To that we now return.

Master/disciple patterns today

We can establish between members of our congregation various parallels to the Jesus/disciple pattern. A disciple watches and listens as his master speaks. He questions what he doesn't understand and he emulates the master's life. Paul asked those in the churches to whom he wrote to follow him in just that way. The underlying concept is quite clear. It means: the young learning from the old, the immature from the mature, the spiritually shallow from the spiritually deep and the easily tempted from the less easily tempted. It assumes that there are deeply mature Christian men and women willing to share their lives and that there are younger disciples wanting to learn.

Suppose I am between nineteen and twenty-four years and wanting to sort out, in a thoroughgoing way, what being a Christian disciple means in today's world. I might go to live with an experienced older person and his or her family for a year or more as a deliberate spiritual education and as part of my "emancipation" from my parents. That could be much more edifying, though maybe much harder than living in a group of peers in a dorm or an apartment where problems are often aggravated, not solved.

The peer group has its place. Who would want to stop the youth clubs and all the rest? Not I, unless there was some other good reason. But peer grouping can be exaggerated. Ranging from pre-kindergarten playgroups to retirement villages, does it not dominate our existence outside the nuclear family and nullify any learning or living experience across the generations? Within the church this pattern is also uncritically copied, as is seen by Sunday Schools, Bible classes, mothers' and older citizens' groups.

Charlie, a fellow staff worker in student Christian work, used to bemoan the lack of time spent by Christian elders (ecclesiastical and chronological) with their young men and women. He met hundreds of students and became familiar with many churches. He often said how rare it was for a Christian student to get even half an hour of unbroken or unstolen time from an older person, for a really good chat about matters important at that time to the student. He laid the blame on the elders—although he wouldn't excuse the younger people—who were so *private* in their whole way of life, so *busy* with their families, houses, gardens, recreation and work that they were rarely able to give the needed chunks of time.

But it does happen. I had a letter from Bill, a young university graduate, thrilled that he was now living with one or two others his own age in the home of a very much older couple. With them he is finding something of the discipling community for which he had been searching. And, to pick up an earlier theme, this couple have to know that such inclusion of young men and women in their lives is appropriate to the time that they are in. But, given that, exciting things can be accomplished.

The details of such plans do not matter. Maybe a regular, two-hour chat over a cup of coffee each Friday night for a year or two would do instead. *Talking* is certainly useful, for there is a multitude of topics to be thrashed out: work, recreation, pleasure and possessions; worship, prayer, spirituality and church structures; various relational and ethical matters both personal and political—and lots of other subjects. The list may read like an informal course in applied theology, but behind it lie the basics of Christian doctrine: revelation, man, God, creation, Christology, the Holy Spirit, discipleship, the kingdom and the church. Even though the people doing the discussing may never actually use any of these names, in theological terms these are the topics they are covering.

But talking on its own, especially if it's spasmodic, doesn't answer the real need of young Christians. *Role models* are also desperately required. And the relationship must not be distant. It must be close enough for the younger to see the older person living out his or her faith in the heat and pressure of daily life.

Let us not misunderstand. When we talk about paralleling our Lord's disciple pattern, we are not imagining for a moment virtuous lives free from all blemish, hung out for others to admire. Failure, sin and the inevitable credibility gap there will be on occasions, as well as saintliness, obedience and joy. No disciple of Christ would claim to be as Christ himself. Moreover, critical following is required, not slavish imitation or the development of a guru mentality. What is urgently needed is more and more openness and less and less seclusion from older disciples who are genuinely wrestling with being a Christian in today's world. University-level articulateness or intellectual knowledge is not necessarily needed. Older Christians need to share their questions and their answers by letting their lives be seen. And as they explain, as they listen to comments from their younger friends, they will find themselves provoked to more study, more regular prayer and more thoroughgoing obedience. "Older" can be as young as twenty-five or as old as seventy plus. Jesus was only thirty and Timothy wasn't exactly ancient!

Late teenagers and early twenties having some close association with older people other than parents is not the only way in which we can approximate the master/disciple relationship. If I am needing a fuller prayer life, regardless of how old I am, could I not ask any person in my congregation, who is vitally alive in those areas, to spend two hours a week with me for two months teaching me (by instruction and practice) about prayer? Or might not married couples talk, more than they do, with engaged couples and newly marrieds about their joys, problems and learning-in-marriage experiences? Because our most common educational environment is the highly organized institution offering large group tuition, these suggestions about learing based on very personal, very open master/disciple relationships almost have a quaint ring. But apparent quaintness should not deter us. Where this kind of persistent, personal learning occurs, it is highly effective.

Of course risk is involved. "Apollos" and "Paul" factions[38] can develop if some people follow one leader and some another. But matters should never reach that stage. Wise pastoral oversight within the church should prevail and people be sensitive to the possibility of conflicting loyalties developing—and deal with them before they get out of hand. In any case, if not just one or two prominent people, but many maturing Christians are encouraging, admonishing and coaxing people who need their help, the development of a divisive party spirit will be thrwarted before it ever begins. Such a pattern is healthy as well as therapeutic. The one leader/one flock type of Christian leadership is the mark of a weak, not a mature fellowship, and the breeding ground for forms of psychological dependency more characteristic of the cults than the New Testament church.

Dull conformity

What we are really examining under the title "privacy" are symptoms of the increasingly rampant creed of individualism, and Christian borrowings from it. But these cannot be examined without raising a seemingly contradictory trend, the trend towards conformity. Several signs clearly indicate this. One is the move towards "collectivism," about which C. S. Lewis made pertinent Christian comment as long ago as 1945.[39] Compare the use of collective labels such as "senior citizens", "teenagers" or "factory workers". These are a great convenience to the ad man and to anyone else who wishes to group people in order to then use, abuse or dismiss them.

Another sign is the greater and greater intrusion of "regulations," most of them petty, into daily life. If you want to build a house you can, provided you conform strictly to specifications about foundations, pipes, stairs, sinks, wiring, side yards, back yards and a thousand other particulars. Some of this is to ensure safety and fair dealing but, whether it is or is not, it is still intervention which imposes conformity. You only notice the restrictions when you don't want to conform. As soon as you depart from the usual, the long arm of the State of the local council taps you gently on the shoulder.

A third symptom is the retention, often by computer bank, of more and more *information* about individuals. A recent informal list made by someone in the computer business counted up to forty data bases on which names of ordinary citizens may well appear.[40] These range over such things, as gas companies, magazine subscriptions, sports licenses, banks, finance companies, income tax, census and electoral rolls. And many of these storage systems are interconnected. All of this means that someone knows a lot about you and me—knowledge which in itself is a pressure to conformity, by appearing as a threat to individual freedom and individuality.

Are these moves towards conformity attempts to cope with individualism? I think so, and therefore they are not so much contradictory as complementary. Rampant individualism ends in anarchy, so the more choice there is, the more authorities regulate in a frantic attempt to keep everything together. "All dog owners will . . ."—there is a collective label. And all the legislation about where or where not dogs can run, excrete and urinate, when or when not they will be dosed for ticks and what license tag they will wear are instances of regulations infiltrating more and more aspects of private life. And of course the dogs and their owners' names are—third symptom—on informations lists. All this is done to cope with potential as well as actual interference to others, and with the chaos and ill health that would result. In short, others' individual rights are protected by restricting mine. Developing individualism leads to developing conformity.

Is the plea made in this chapter for less sociological and individual privacy, but more corporate Christian life in reality a plea for conformity? Are Christians merely using collective labels (like "Christian young people"), intrusive regulations (like daring to talk about how people should live) and storage of information (like knowledge acquired in a small group life) to press people into a servile conformity as members of a subgroup in the wider society?

A two-way life

Just as Christian teaching insists on corporate life, so it insists on the individuality of those who come together. Paul speaks many times of different gifts and functions within the body of Christ, the church.[41] Jesus himself chose a varied bunch for his closest twelve, including fishermen, a tax gatherer, a political fanatic and the quiet, gentle Andrew.[42] The church in any given locality is lame—less than whole—if some individual is absent. There is a qualitative as well as a quantitative loss when someone leaves. And there is at the very heart of the gospel the question of individual response to the teaching, atoning death and resurrection of Jesus. That response in faith leads two ways at once: to individual, "with God" privacy and to life together in a loving, caring fellowship that then turns outwards into sacrificial service for others.

Individualism is contrary to Christian life; individuality is essential to it. *Community*, not conformity, is the Christian ideal. A church should be like a patchwork quilt. The patches are all different but, sewn together, they not only effectively cover the bed, but create a sheer, bright harmony of conglomerate color which cheers everyone who walks into the room. It even attracts those who look in through the window.

4
Means & ends

The thesis of this chapter is essentially simple: the societies in which we live are dominated by technical means. Christians living in these societies, both individually and as the corporate church, are likewise dominated, usually without realizing it. This domination inhibits those of us who are Christian from being what we should be. We first need to see what is happening and, secondly, plan how to escape.

By "technical means" I understand all rational, controlled tools and repetitive methods. This is a very wide description, owing much to machines and mechanics. It includes all that we commonly call "technology", flows on to electronics and extends into all of life.

Say, for example, one goes to a supermarket, collects a basket, trundles down the various rows in a certain predetermined pattern (as governed by the overhead labels swinging in the artificial breeze), takes goods to a checkout, puts them on the counter (always the same-shaped counter and the same-size basket in every store), watches the cashier push certain buttons according to her reading of the price tags, collects groceries from the packer and moves out, dumping one's basket in the steel gate by the swing doors—all of that constitutes a domination by technical means.

Or take a worship service in which one is served communion from throw-away wax-paper cups, distributed by tailor-suited, carefully-rehearsed stewards who carry identical wooden or chrome trays. There, technical means are ruling at the heart of Christian celebration.

Or again, one climbs into a car, pushes and pulls buttons and levers, turns a wheel and off one goes, usually alone, to one's destination.

These examples—and they are only examples—bear further examination. Because we want to buy cheaply and quickly, we go to the supermarket, presumably assuming that cheapness and efficiency are desirable goals. Because the throw-away cups are hygienic, save people having to wash them and are readily available, we use them and stylize that part of the service around the best technique of serving and collecting them afterwards. We even imagine that this quiet, rigid arrangement has something to do with reverence. And the car? We will keep that for separate treatment later![1]

Our preoccupation with means

Of the dominance of technical means there are thousands of illustrations, both general and everyday, which are common to most people. The word "thousands" is important. You may be shaking your head, thinking that I am making mountains out of molehills or crying "wolf" when there is no danger. But, although most of the examples which we can give are trivial, it's the continual agglomeration of all of these trivia which constitutes the preoccupation with technical means. We just don't realize how dominated we are.

My wife is a doctor. At times when she has been in general

practice she has received protests, spoken or unspoken, from patients who were not satisfied with being sent away without a prescription for medicine. An explanation, that the patient had a virus against which there are as yet no drugs or that slow recovery by bed rest was necessary for full health, did not satisfy. So common and so effective are antibiotics, steroids, sedatives, anti-depressants and sleeping pills over actual symptoms that the patient has come to think that these are always a short-cut to health. We might almost say that a patient comes to a doctor to get pills rather than to get well! Means are well on the way to replacing ends.

Sometimes I have been asked to someone's house to hear their stereo. The lightness of the pickup, the output of the amplifier, the frequency range (should I have brought my dog?) and the mahogany grain of the cabinet take precedence over the King's Singers, the New Zealand Symphony Orchestra, Abba or the Fisher Folk and what they sing or play. The means have replaced the ends.

A friend came home from a long stint in a country in the Third World. He had been in charge of health care for people scattered throughout remote villages in valleys, each one of which had a different language. He told with frustration and evident despair of a centralized hospital erected in his area by one of the wealthy Western nations. It had stainless steel benches, modern filing systems, up-to-date X-ray facilities, an initially well-equipped pharmacy and many other technological delights . . . and the inbuilt expectation that people would suddenly change their lifestyle and travel long distances to the hospital.

The institution was welcomed by the receiving government, but very quickly became useless because it had not the trained staff to run it, nor the local equipment and services to replenish and repair it. The wonder of technological achievement had run away with the planners. Means had become ends, and the ends were useless.

From all spheres of life—private, institutional, ecclesiastical, business, agricultural and governmental—there are countless examples of means becoming ends. And therein lies the sadness: instances abound. To note them is not to allocate blame or suggest superior knowledge, but to alert ourselves to what surrounds us and demands our active reflection. Society in general has largely lost sight of goals, ends or purpose. Technical means have taken over; they have become ends in themselves.

Some implications

Conforming to this terrible tyranny of means brings serious consequences. First there is a lessening of time and energy given to deeper human fraternization.

This statement needs explaining. The availability of increasingly efficient technical means in the field of communication increases and diversifies human contact. A bus driver meets many more people than ever his predecessor did with a horse and cart. A business executive, travelling the globe by air, spends time with a far greater range of people on one three-week trip than his more sedentary predecessor did in as many years. Any ordinary telephone subscriber, equipped with a directory, has immediate contact with thousands of people all over the world. His or her number of contacts increases, but the depth of contact is likely to diminish. As telecommunications advance, televised business conferences by satellite or coaxial cable between people in different locations will become commonplace; social get-togethers on the same TV screens may follow. The contact will be immediate, but passing—the relationships more numerous but more temporary.

Interpersonal communications can be thought of as a series of concentric circles, with the individual standing in the center. The different circles represent the different depths and range of social contact any one individual has. Allowing for some variations between people, the modern urban citizen has much more contact with the outer circles than did his predecessors. But probably he has much less with the inner two circles, those which represent his friends and family. Even if he has now the same "inner circle" relationships as he did twenty years ago, the outside circles have so increased in influence that in terms of percentages he is overwhelmed by the more cursory contacts.

Second, there is an emphasis on things, both abstract (e.g., efficiency) and material (e.g., cars). Moreover we have already seen that affluence pushes us in this direction.[2]

Third, there is an elided view of love and service in that technical means, while aiming at efficiency, often neglect caring and serving which may, in fact, demand inefficiency. Thus the wax-paper cups are certainly efficient and hygienic. But could it be that more joy, more love, more genuine celebration, more symbolic service to each other would result from the congregation gathering in several parts of the church building, each group around a hand-crafted goblet made by an amateur potter in the congregation, administering the elements to each other while singing psalms and spiritual songs—after the style prescribed by Paul in his letter to the Ephesians?[3] Have we buried the purpose of the Lord's Supper—deep fellowship with God and with each other—in the very method of conducting it?

Fourth, there is a misplaced emphasis on "activity" as the stuff of life. Because "we are able to", "we do" and because we are able to do "more and more efficiently", we do "more and more". Hence life is a whirl of one thing following another with accompanying noise! Silence and inactivity make today's Westerners terribly uncomfortable.[4] There is not much room for being still and knowing that the Lord is God.[5]

Fifth, because technical research, application and construction become each day more and more perfect, something arranged, bought or made yesterday is soon thought less perfect. So the people who bought "yesterday" feel a very strong urge within to replace it with the latest model— and so the "new is better" syndrome asserts itself. Its clinical signs are (for those seeking an early diagnosis) dissatisfaction, gruff looks at present equipment, wistful delving into catalogues and a predeliction to listen to salespeople!

Technical means create their own forward dynamic, which is very difficult to contain. Trying to hold on is like trying to stop a runaway car on a hill by braking with one foot, while standing on the accelerator with the other. Technical means are running rampant although most people, especially those who develop them, are reluctant to admit this is the case. Jacques Ellul claims that:

> In this terrible dance of means which have been unleashed, no one knows where we are going, the aim of life has been forgotten, the end has been left behind. Man has set out at tremendous speed—to go nowhere.[6]

Some far-reaching possibilities

So far, the examples of the domination of technical means given have been quite ordinary, for instance supermarket techniques. Indeed they are so commonplace that most people have used them without even questioning what has been happening. But during the 1980s we can expect to see one new set of technical means which will radically transform our existence. If adopted, it will bring "the information revolution", "the wired city", "the post-technological society", "the electronic age", "the new automation"—to name some of the labels being applied.[7]

As I write, I have on my desk a 16,000 register computer —at least I have the essence of it. It is a tiny square of silicon no more than one cm across. This "chip", when combined with input and output channels and other facilities, is comparable in processing power to a large computer of the early 1960s. That computer cost thousands of dollars. This chip costs a few cents. Components like it lie at the heart of the technological revolution because of their information-storing ability, their size and their cheapness. The era of the micro-processor is here. What will happen?

Peter Goldmark, well-known inventor and electronic communications developer, foresees a new future in which the population in the USA will increasingly live in rural townships, in houses electronically connected to every other house. His electronic network:

> can be looked upon as providing a pipe into every home, office or library through which one can not only converse but also transmit and receive written materials, pictures, data etc.[8]

Philip Lapp, a Canadian expert, in a comprehensive survey of communications technology, lists over sixty home services that could be provided by a house terminal, linked by cable TV to computers. He has a whole host of suggested services under various headings such as: shopping and merchandizing, general information services (which would include an electronic newspaper, transmitted during the night and ready from the home terminal printout in the morning), community services (for instance theater and restaurant reservations), telemetry and security (which would include automatic reading of the household electric, water and gas meters), person to person communication (including an-

swering services and business conferences) and education
(including self-choice televised home education programs
for adults).

And the list goes on. He is no science fiction purveyor.
At the time of speaking, items on his list were all technologi-
cally possible and many were already being used in trials.
Since then, so fast has been the development rate that some
of the facilities he suggests are already on the market. Lapp
concluded the paper he gave to the science symposium:

> I personally have a great concern about the impact of
> the wired city on people. Will it make them fat and
> lazy, or will it inspire them to higher accomplish-
> ments through the provision of more leisure time for
> creativity? The only thing I feel quite certain about
> is that the technology already is at hand, aggressive
> entrepreneurs will exploit it, and the people must be
> given the freedom of choice either to embrace it or
> reject it. [9]

Some commentators think we will accept all these developments. Others are sure we won't. Dr. Jib Fowles of the
University of Houston, USA, is one observer who thinks
men and women will pass by the non-mobility information
society of the wired city. He claims that the unpopularity
of cable television and videophones in the USA during the
1970s already indicates this. He explains:

> Whatever our age or sex, we humans need a great
> deal of unmediated contact in our lives if we are to
> remain socialized. Those who have been compelled to
> live apart, such as prisoners in solitary confinement,
> testify to how unnerving the experience is; those who
> would make great use of electronic communications in
> their relations with their social environment would

suffer not in degree, but certainly in kind. The sense of deprivation arises from the fact that communication systems must reduce stimuli in order to convey messages efficiently, while we humans are in need of the full spectrum of interpersonal contact during much of our day . . . As much as they might like each other, the members of contemporary families would find it difficult to spend every hour of the day in each other's company. More satisfaction would be likely to result in the present pattern of separation at the day's start and reassembling at the end. [10]

So Fowles speaks for those who think that we will not see a changed way of life as a result of the introduction of the micro-processor.

The rule of "can"

Whether Fowles and others will prove to be correct is a matter which only the future will determine. Nevertheless, I suspect that as the new technology becomes ever more readily available, ever cheaper and more reliable, people, irrespective of education, occupation and social class, will grab it willingly. The other day in a meeting a buzzer sounded. The cleric responsible for the noise rose, apologized and left—to conduct a funeral. The preset time alarm on his calculator had called him.

Who would have thought even ten years ago that pencil-thin calculators would have been in every top pocket, every purse and in many a schoolbag? At the end of World War II, how many people would have predicted the vast air traffic of Westerners—and increasingly Easterners, both "Near" and "Far"—who traverse the world for fun, experience and business? Calculators and travel: they are only two contemporary examples of how technical means have dramatically changed patterns of human behavior. On the basis of such precedents it is clear we need to be cautious, reflective and discerning about forthcoming changes.

Sir Ieuan Maddock, secretary of the British Association for the Advancement of Science, in emphasizing just how all-pervasive and powerfully influential the new technology will be, has said it "will extend or even displace man's capacity for thinking, his intuition or his judgment". He called the new technology "the most remarkable mankind has ever designed".[11] Are we not likely to accept new means just because they are here? There is no doubt that governments and other power groupings take this potential revolution very seriously. Look for instance at Australia's National Telecommunications Planning Group, an elite squad which sits at the very top of the huge Post Office bureaucracy. It's unlike anything Australia has ever seen before, and its concern is the future shape of the information society in that country.[12]

The new technology, because of the magnitude and rapidity of change, only sharpens and makes more urgent the issues raised by our consideration of technical means in general. Therefore we now return to the central thesis. We may think of the problem this way. "We do it because we can", says modern technological man, not "We do it because we ought". At nearly every point in life, pragmatic possibilities replace imperatives based on goals. A "we can—let's do it" attitude dominates a tremendous portion of our present as well as our future, where "we can" includes "we can afford it". Affluence reinforces the dominance of means. Should Christians let "can" (or "can't") rule?

What ought we to do?

Here are five suggestions:

(a) We should deliberately make prayer a part of our technological analysis.

As technique marches resolutely on its way, there is nothing trite about asking God to give us insight. So useful are technical means, so close do we stand to what they can do for us, that often we do not see the consequences—whether good or bad. Take an example from the imminent future.

Do we want to live in "houses that think"?[13] Such houses have at their heart computers linked to switches and communication devices which regulate, check, inventory and order everything from TV video-cassettes to room lights, from theater tickets to groceries on the pantry shelf, from the temperature of the oven to the temperature of the goldfish bowl. Such houses, if cheap and commonplace in the future, will obviously be more convenient than houses in which we live now—assuming that they draw energy from plentiful and renewable resources such as the sun.

The full range of social consequences however is difficult to predict, both for those who will live in them and for those who won't. Will boredom increase? Will people successfully fill their newfound leisure hours? Will interpersonal communication thrive or suffocate? And what about privacy— will the fences continue to rise with the salary scales? The list of possible developments is endless. When faced with such far-reaching technical means and consequent social change, we certainly need human caution amplified by divine insight!

(b) We should devote time to further serious study and reading, both individually and in groups.

What we need to study first are theological answers to our preoccupation with means. To do this we must come to terms with who we are as Christians. This necessitates re-examining what Christ did, because he makes us who we are. Jacques Ellul again gives insight:

> *The point from which we ought to start is that, in the work of God, the end and the means are identical. Thus when Jesus Christ is present, the kingdom has "come upon" us. This formula expresses very precisely the relation between the end and the means. Jesus Christ in his incarnation appears as God's means for the salvation of man and for the establishment of the kingdom of God but, where Jesus Christ is, there also is his salvation and his kingdom.* [14]

And where is Jesus? In the lives of those who are understanding and following him. Their lives are part of the kingdom. Their lives are part of the "end". [15] They are "means" too, but means only of manifesting, declaring, showing or demonstrating that end, that kingdom.

As a consequence of all this, Christians are not to use technical means unless these means remain quite firmly subservient. Christians need to realize that they are "people of the end"! Unless this theological insight is grasped, we have no chance of finding a base for determining whether or not acceptance of any particular technical means is warranted. Rather we will tend easily to lose our way amongst the galaxy of attractively pervasive gadgets and methodologies.

But Christians are to be "means" as well! The Christian, in living true to Christ who is both the means and the end, is to be a footwasher to fellow Christians and a good Samaritan to others—a servant to all! To the extent that any technical means can enhance that service, they ought to be used. But in thinking theologically about this servant role, we need to see it as requiring genuine love and human response. It is not just a matter of efficiency, but of self-sacrificial service done in obedience to him who served us and gave his life as a ransom for many.[16]

(c)   *We should share ways in which our theological and tech-
      nological study, when applied to today's situation, can
      show itself in our moral attitudes and everyday lifestyle.*

Once our theological base is established, we can begin to
evaluate various situations from a technological viewpoint.
We must look at particulars, including the examples we have
used in this chapter. It is not trivial to decide what to do
about supermarkets and corner stores. It is not silly to try
and think through our attitude to Goldberg's interconnected
small communities. It's certainly right to think about the
influence of the new technology upon work.[17] We need to
apply our perception to how society should be structured
to the nitty-gritty of technological change, not let research
and development units of transnational corporations set the
social agenda.

(d)   *We should start doing small, practical things to make
      technology our servant, not our master.*

Why not start by switching off our television and going to
watch the neighbors'; then, when we've established human
contact, persuade them to switch theirs off so that we can
talk to them! Or we can write to manufacturers, distributors,
retailers and government agencies who seem entrapped by
means, to make our protest and suggestions about how, for
instance, they can make their products more serviceable,
durable and less gimmicky. We can grow things, either in
window boxes, indoor pots or gardens, as we need them.
There are thousands of small, practical but significant things
that we can do which will show that we will use technical
means, but not be controlled by them.

(e)   *In every work and recreational situation, whether class-*

*room, business, factory, office or church—wherever we
are—we should think very carefully before we take on
some new technical means.*

We will ask ourselves: "What will it do to us? What will
it do to our families? What will it do to our employees, fellow
union members, customers, pupils or clients? What will it
do to our congregations?" And then we will scrutinize ourselves carefully as to whether or not we are simply capitulat-
ing to a new technique which is available, rather than being
sure that we know (and agree with) the end that it is meant
to serve.

There may be other answers to the question, "What ought
we to do?" We are in the midst of a time of solid debate
whether we know it or not. Glib answers and facile solutions
are of little use. So strong is the tyranny of means that our
demand to decide for ourselves how we will live, rather than
acquiesce to someone else's manipulation, is likely to lead
us into pain and even self-doubt. But that is part of the price
to be paid for a life of Christian integrity in the post-technological society.

Shall we all be primitive?

To write as I have written in this chapter sometimes causes
confusion. "What is all this really about? Are we to throw
away rehearsed methods, typed agendas, washing machines,
calculators, computers and electronic communications? Are
we to go back to squatting, eating raw meat in a candle-lit
room before a fire in a mud hut?"

No! Being Christian doesn't mean being primitive, although it probably does mean fewer washing machines
bought (as more are shared) and certainly fewer machines
sold on the basis of a few extra gadgets. It may mean fewer
calculators, particularly for school children who are learning

basic mathematics. It will mean asking a lot of hard "why" questions, before deciding a computer is necessary and desirable in this or that situation. It may mean being content with less instant communications, particularly when stress is caused by the speed and volume of those communications. But, although these questions are fair, both questions and answers miss the central thrust of living Christianly over and against the dominance of means—at least if asked as the main response to what we've been discussing.

Our response to the dominance of technical means will not be a nostalgic one: to return to an earlier culture, whether first century, sixteenth or nineteenth—at home to use candles instead of electric light, in the hospital to use guesswork instead of laboratory tests, in the factory to use hand instead of mechanical or electrical power. Rather our response will be a cognitive one: to realize who we are and to construct a lifestyle (both personal and professional) which consciously and consistently puts the qualities of the kingdom ahead of any other articulated or unspoken pragmatic ideology. In the living out of this lifestyle technical means, of whatever kind, must be held firmly under control. If they change roles from "servant" to "master", they will be considered recalcitrant. If they move from being useful tools to becoming works of art for their own sake, they will have usurped their rightful place. If they shift from controlled means to ends to be sought at all costs, they must be rebuked and disciplined. Technology was made for man, not man for technology.

Technical means are welcome so long as they remain servants. For instance, an office won't hesitate to use a recall or data-retention system. To do so is to reflect the design of the God of order, not chaos. But an office in which Christians make such managerial decisions will not introduce systems which, while they may be efficient, make no real contribution to human service and care which the office is supposed to provide. Such managers will fight tooth and nail—graciously!—to prevent the installation of methods and machinery which cause unnecessary redundancy or emotional tension, or the proliferation of gadgets which have no real purpose. They will not place means over ends. They will not let "can" rule.

And what is true in the work of office managers will be true of every aspect of life. Of course the amount of authority varies. In personal and family life there is more possibility of seeing the "results on the ground" than in a big corporation, an ecclesiastical institution or a political organization. But even in those larger and more frightening spheres, where Christians may constitute only small minorities denied real sovereignty, the light needs to shine[18] and the salt rub sore.[19]

Standing firm

Probably the hardest thing for us to do will be to challenge the status quo. We are so used to taking for granted technical means that some may wonder if it is even proper to question their place in life.[20] To make matters worse, we will be told that we are mixing things up—bringing questions and values from one realm (Christian faith) into another (technical and sociological change), where they have no place to be. Yet this is the very point at which we need to make our strongest stand. We must insist that, if we live in the kingdom in this world and if God is Lord of all, our Christian faith and values touch *every* aspect of life. They are part of the facts of life. With a wry grin which acknowledges that we realize others are free to disagree,[21] and with ongoing good humor which springs from joy in our relationship to God, we will stand our ground—and keep on standing.

5
Mobility

The man sitting next to me was going home from church, taking with him a youth who seemed to have no place to stay—a good thing to be doing after eating Sunday lunch with friends from the congregation. He was a regular church-goer he told me. He missed an occasional Sunday, but not many.

"Tremendous church", he said. "The teaching is terrific, the pastor anointed, the congregation escalating!" We were on a flight from New Zealand's biggest city, Auckland, to the capital, Wellington, and he was changing to another plane to travel to a small South Island town. Altogether his trip to church stretched 500 air miles each way. Today he had travelled on his own, but frequently he took the family. Now and then he combined weekend church with business on Friday or Monday, but often the trip was for church alone. Mobility! He may be unusual. He is certainly the only person I've met who *flies* 500 miles each week to worship. But I know some who drive thirty miles, many who travel across the city and a lot who spend fifteen minutes in their cars between house and church building. Those who walk to worship are comparatively few. We go to church as we might go for a picnic. If there is "a good place" nearby then "okay", but if not then "travel"!

We must delineate and examine the mobility of our era

because it affects Christians pointedly, not only in this simple matter of choosing a church and travelling to it, but in many other far-reaching ways.

Modern migrations

Mobility ("transience" he called it) was one of the major factors with which Alvin Toffler wanted to shock the world in 1970. He had no trouble finding startling statistics. For instance he discovered that in one year 108 million Americans took 360 million trips involving overnight stays more than 100 miles from home. These trips alone accounted for 321,000 million passenger miles.[1]

Moving, changing suburb, adapting to a new city—these are also very significant aspects of the mobility of our times. Commentators call it "geographical" or "relocation mobility". Toffler again popularized what was happening in the USA in the late sixties. In one year, he says, 36.6 million people (not counting infants under one) moved. Each year one out of every five Americans changed residential address.[2]

What huge, massive mobility! As we might expect not all countries match that, but everywhere movement is immense. Take Australia for example. Distances between the major population centers there are vast and, with figures of 14.25 million in 1978, the population is comparatively small.[3] Therefore we might expect little movement, but still surveys of internal migration show that of people over fifteen years of age 1,200,000 (or 15 to 17 percent) changed residence in 12 months.[4] That's a lot of shifting of furniture! And it's interesting to note that for the year ending January 1977, 59 percent of those were in the age range of twenty to thirty-four years.[5]

International and intercontinental travel has boomed,

adding to both temporary and permanent resettlement needs. Barbara Ward and Rene Dubos, quoting United Nations figures, say that whereas in the mid 1950s 51 million tourists arrived in some sixty to seventy countries, by the mid sixties this figure had risen to over 157 million.[6] An interesting sidelight is the great predeliction people have for sunshine, sea and mountains, with ancient ruins thrown in—hence the popularity of countries such as Greece, where the number of tourists trebled in three years.[7] More recent information shows that the trend continues upwards, with only a few undulations in the graph. Hong Kong, still famous as a transit shopping stop, received 1,292,000 people in 1973, but 1,560,000 in 1976,[8] while the United Kingdom, increasingly a Mecca for citizens of every country, saw its tourist inflow rise from 7,724,000 in 1973 to 10,089,000 in 1976.[9]

But it's not all tourism. In 1979 New Zealand, a small country with a total population just over 3 million, *lost* 19,680 New Zealand residents who departed permanently. Add to them all long-term migration and the figure reaches 40,000[10]—the size of a smaller city. Permanent migration features elsewhere too. Australia, like New Zealand one of the newer "Western countries", has perhaps the most interesting figures of all:

> *In the post-war years some 3.47 million migrants have arrived, of which an estimated 80 percent settled. They and those of their children born in Australia have been responsible for about half of Australia's post-war population growth.*[11]

And as people move from diverse language and cultural groups (Africa, America, Europe, Asia, Oceania),[12] just think of the adjustments that have to be made. Not only are newer countries affected. In 1976 210,000 people emigrated from Britain mainly to Australia, New Zealand and Canada, but also to fellow-member countries of the European Economic Community. Then, in the same year, Britain received 180,000 immigrants—mostly from British Commonwealth countries.[13] Similar figures can be repeated in all the more affluent nations.

Whoever moves has to cope with new neighbors, shops, school, tennis club, doctor and transport services (when present!) *all at once*. International settlers often have to adjust to new languages, political philosophies, food, cultures and religious backgrounds. If the settlers are Christians they have to adjust to a new church as well—and the church to them. What a flux! A comment Toffler made in 1970 is truer now than when he originally offered it:

> *Never in history has distance meant less. Never have man's relationships with place been more numerous, fragile and temporary. Throughout the advanced technological societies, and particularly among those I have characterized as "the people of the future", commuting, travelling and regularly relocating one's family have become second nature. Figuratively, we "use up" places and dispose of them in much the same way that we dispose of Kleenex or beer cans. We are witnessing a historic decline in the significance of place to human life. We are breeding a new race of nomads, and few suspect quite how massive, widespread and significant their migrations are.[14]*

And what is the significance of this massive nomadicy for Christians, both for themselves and for those with whom they live and work? What are some of the far-reaching ways which affect them? Perhaps the best way to approach this is to focus on Christians gathered in any local church.

Living in the church

David Thorns, in *Suburbia* which draws from first-level research in North America and the United Kingdom, notices that high geographical mobility families are grouped together in suburbs, having previously cut themselves off from traditional kinship ties. He observes that many of the middle-class highly mobile in particular seem keen to be in churches, probably not from any specifically religious desires so much as to make community contacts to overcome the isolation which is part of newness. He recognizes that churches in the the middle-class suburbs seem to be highly organized like the rest of middle-class life and, again, it may be affinity with that activity for its own sake rather than religious motivation which makes churches there popular. Evidence also shows that it is out of concern for their children that these middle-class suburban mobiles are often church-goers.[15]

But a local church—*ekklesia* in the New Testament, meaning "assembly of called ones"—is meant to be more than a sociological grouping which provides neighborhood socials and services, activities which Rotary or a children's playgroup could do better. An *ekklesia* theologically is a corporate body, a community of the forgiven, its members united by their worship of God the Father, Son and Holy Spirit. Part of the outworking of this kind of lifestyle we have already discussed while investigating privacy.

Insight into contemporary church character comes from our everyday speech. "Which church do you attend?" we ask, or "Which church do you go to?" These questions give the impression that church is in some way outside the rest of life. We leave what we are doing or where we are living and "go to" or "attend" church. And we go to participate in a communion service, hear the preacher or take the kids to Sunday school—or to do something else which we describe in terms of activity. Now and then we speak of church as an entity to which we *belong* and, sometimes, as a place in which we *work*. We say, "My church work keeps me busy on Sundays", or "He works hard running the Bible class". "Belong" is probably the best of all those words, because it is the only one which expresses permanent, intimate relationship. That relationship might be strengthened further if we speak not of "belonging to", but of "living in" the church.

"Living in the church" need not be thought a strange idea. As a way of expressing the deep, mutual responsibility to each other found in sharing joy, worship, suffering, service and fellowship as taught in the Pauline letters especially, it has a lot to recommend it. For example, in Colossians chapter 2 we read that Paul wanted Christians in the churches for which he had some pastoral responsibility to be "knit together in love", provided their "assured understanding" was in Christ "in whom are hid all the treasures of wisdom and knowledge". They were to "live in him" and he was to be the center of the church. By "holding fast" to him they, as the body, were to be "nourished and knit together through its joints and ligaments", to grow "with a growth that is from God".[16] If members of congregations today put themselves in the place of the Colossians, thus allowing Paul to address them, they would find that concentration together upon Christ results in a great, harmonious linking of one another for the purpose of growing—and it is that linked-together growth to which we are giving expression when we "live in the church".

This concept of "living in the church" should not be dismissed on the grounds that a church with this aim is likely to become a ghetto or a clique. In service and in spreading "all that Jesus began to do and teach",[17] the church is directed outwards from its fellowship together. A church, aware of the danger of inwardness, can avoid it by constant checking. We are helped in this task if we remind ourselves that we live in the kingdom of God solely by virtue of our acknowledgment and following of Jesus. The kingdom and the church are thus linked in proclamation. The relationship of church to kingdom has often been debated, but we seem to be standing on strong biblical ground in agreeing with George Eldon Ladd that:

> The kingdom of God, as the redemptive activity and rule of God and Christ, created the church and works through the church in the world. . . In the same way, the kingdom of God, the redemptive activity and power of God, is working in the world today through the church of Jesus Christ. The church is the fellowship of disciples of Jesus who have received the life of the kingdom and are dedicated to the task of preaching the gospel of the kingdom in the world. Philip went to Samaria preaching "good news about the kingdom of God and the name of Jesus Christ" (Acts 8:12). Paul went to Rome and preached first to the Jews, then to the Gentiles, the kingdom of God (Acts 28:23,31).[18]

A church is clearly meant to be both close-knit, as it loves and cares for its members, and outward-looking, as it constantly turns outwards to share the gospel.

Living in the church would be a whole lot easier if we reduced our mobility. Barbara Ward describes the private car as "the answer to all mismatches of employment, residence and recreation.[19] We could extend the list by adding "church", or by moving it from her implicit inclusion under "recreation" to a separate category more befitting its importance. To live in a church is to be known and recognized, waved to from windows or street, greeted in shops, visited for conversation, prayer and coffee, specifically encouraged in devotional life and helped with tax returns, a broken fence or your child's piano lessons. And it is to reciprocate similarly. Living in the church also provides an environment in which guidance comes about matters in one's own life, and the lives of others, as the church says "It seemed good to the Holy Spirit and to us".[20] It is a place in which, as a result of both individual and corporate worship, one grows in holiness.

For a church to be all of that, its people should not live a long way from their place of meeting and from each other. Indeed, misplacement and consequent car travel can easily be an escape from problems in relationships and hence from growth in the quality of the corporate life of the congregation. One of the people with whom I live commented: "We *have* to solve our problems. We *have* to grow more understanding, accepting and helping because we live here. We can't run away." How simply said—but the implications are powerfully immense.

Shall we move?

Not only Sunday car travel, but frequent moving affects directly the well-being of a church. The trend to frequent relocation is certainly psychologically and culturally disturbing for most people, although some seem to thrive initially by each change of locale. But even if it were not disturbing, on purely Christian grounds shouldn't it be resisted? How can a congregation grow together and "turn outwards", unless its members live together for a considerable time in the region where they minister? Especially as we have to cope anyway with a sociological trend to privacy and isolation, do we not need ample time to visit each other, know each other, care for each other and make decisions together?

I have lived for eight years in my church—a small one by many standards, with a nominal roll of 450 families and a worshipping core of 100 adults in a suburb which, because of geographical shape and history, retains the feel of a village —but I am still gaining new insights and discovering new people. In an age when relocation mobility is high and probably increasing, those who see the difficulties so produced need to minister to those for whom mobility necessitates rapid adjustment and all its associated problems. That demands a core of people dedicated to following Christ who *stay* in one place—and that applies to every sort of residential situation. It is a message to be heard by those in urban centers, old suburbs, new suburbs, dormitory towns, housing estates and country areas.

Place does have biblical significance. Adam and Eve were put in a garden, then driven from it after sinning.[21] Jacob and his sons were led by Joseph's saga to Egypt[22] and then, at God's direction, their descendants were moved ultimately to the promised land.[23] Jerusalem had a special significance for the people of Israel[24] and later the disciples, after the crucifixion and resurrection, were told to stay in that city until the Holy Spirit came.[25] Paul in his journeys was conscious of the divine intervention in determining when and where he should come and go.[26] As Christians today therefore, we do violence to the biblical perspective if we see the place we live in as purely determined by work, pleasure or financial advantage. In the Scriptures a called people had a *given* place for a *particular* time. That is a notion we must hold to tenaciously.

There's another more subtle point. Does the very transience of society cause low expectations among Christians of the achievable dimensions of fellowship? I won't try very hard to make meaningful relationships which, in three years time or less, will be broken. Even further, if I'm used to moving frequently I probably have never experienced a deep dimension of fellowship. Therefore when people talk to me about biblical ideas of a caring community instituted by Jesus, I will find it very difficult to visualize anything deeper than what I've known. I will be prohibited by my experiences from appreciating what is being suggested. In fact I'll even be inclined to dismiss any who share deeply and live closely as being "a bit funny"! Astonishing. The norm of society has become the norm for the church.

Your humble, obedient tourist servants

And how do we regard tourist mobility? Do we accept it, take part in it, protest against it, encourage it? We have already noticed what a large factor it is in our mobile life.

Perhaps the severest criticism of tourist travel is to be made on financial grounds. Do we have any right to spend so much money on "going to look" while so many people live on such low levels of existence? Indeed we may be "going to look" at some of those very people as though they were in some kind of exhibition. Or we may be feeding the coffers of the rich who keep them poor—depending on where we go. In terms of either support of fellow Christians or giving to the poor, spending of our affluence just to "go and look" seems very hard to justify. And why do we "go" anyway? To a large extent is not tourist travel just a cult of our times?

Art Buchwald has caught this aspect cheekily and amusingly in his Tourists' Prayer:

> *Heavenly Father, look down on us your humble obedient tourist servants who are doomed to travel this earth taking photographs, mailing postcards, buying souvenirs and walking around in drip-dry*

underwear. We beseech you, O Lord, to see that our plane is not hijacked, our luggage is not lost and our overweight baggage goes unnoticed.

Give us this day divine guidance in our selection of hotels. We pray that the phones work, that the operators speak our tongue and there is no mail waiting from our children that would force us to cancel the rest of our trip.

Lead us to good, inexpensive restaurants where the wine is included in the price of the meal. Give us the wisdom to tip correctly in currencies we do not understand. Make the natives love us for what we are and not for what we can contribute to their worldly goods. Grant us the strength to visit the museums, the cathedrals, the palaces and if, perchance, we skip a historic monument to take a nap after lunch, have mercy on us, for our flesh is weak.

Dear God, protect our wives from bargains they don't need or can't afford. Lead them not into temptation for they know not what they do.

Almighty Father, keep our husbands from looking at foreign women and comparing them to us. Save them from making fools of themselves in nightclubs. Above all, please do not forgive them their trespasses for they know exactly what they do.

And when our voyage is over, grant us the favor of finding someone who will look at our home movies and listen to our stories, so our lives as tourists will not have been in vain. This we ask you in the name of Conrad Hilton, Thomas Cook and the American Express.

Amen.[27]

It speaks for itself, doesn't it.

Yet clearly the enjoyment of scenery, cultural achievements or meeting people is not to be despised. Indeed, as we will see in chapter 7, it is to be encouraged. Would anyone begrudge a family a train trip, with a swim and a picnic at the end of it? How about a holiday in the country half-a-day's journey away, or a Sunday afternoon visit to an art gallery or sports ground? Perhaps it is in the level of mobility suggested by these examples that we need to find our attitude to tourist travel. It is the expenditure of *gross* effort, emotion, time and money upon "going to look" that seems so far from any biblical dimension associated with following Jesus.

All travel is not being discounted. There are real reasons for visiting in the spheres of church life, family obligation, business, recreation and education—though fewer I suspect than are usually advanced. I look at the leather brief-cases walking out of airports and I wonder why their firms find it necessary to send them all overseas. I gaze at the assembled papers and Bibles at a Christian conference and I ponder the delegates' total travel cost. How many mouths would they feed, wells dig or pastors train? But there are still real reasons for travel—we must grant that!

The level of honesty of perception has to be considered too. Tourists are inclined to receive an ersatz view of the society they visit. There is a facade contributed to by both viewer and viewed, at least in the more popular places. The tourist expects certain things, so certain things are provided. Partial reality only is being seen. What values are we perpetuating by participation as consumers in the tourist industry?

Distraction

Moreover, caught in "go-see" mobility, we are continually

"somewhere else". A former colleague of mine says we live in a distracted society. He contends that because of our great mobility and the accompanying ease of communication, there is a tremendous tendency for us never to be "fully present". We are distracted by visits from acquaintances, letters from the past, the anticipation or dread of next weekend's trip, announcements of distant attractions and vague thoughts that "foreign experience is good for us". Because we know we're off on holiday to Europe tomorrow, we are half there today. Because our older children all drive cars, we are worrying about them as they roam over half a city, province or state. Such distraction is antithetical to deep Christian fellowship or ministry to others—even to everyday effective work.

A calling to stay in the one place

Living close together and refusing to conform to the travel cult does not, by itself, produce loving relationships. Those adjacent can be just as distant as those apart. But living closer at least facilitates contact. If Christians are intent upon caring for and being cared for, they can use geographical proximity and undistracted residential long-staying to great advantage. What a tremendous transformation in church life there could be if all Christians resolved to live in their congregational area and move very seldom—only indeed when the congregation sends them! Just think of the potential for ministry of both comfort and challenge in a shift-strained world.

Staying in one place is not easy. As we noticed in the preceding chapter on technical means, trends have their own dynamics.[28] If most people move, I move. It's not easy to stand against the tide. If the pattern is to move every two or three years until I reach the age of forty plus, when I may have reached the limits of my job promotion or found my dream house, then that's what I am likely to do. If most people take their long vacations and "go around the world" or travel here or there for expensive holidays, again that's what I'm likely to do. The social pressure to conform, built up over my whole life, is enormous. It is far higher than many people are prepared to grant. Yet concerning either temporary or permanent moves Christians frequently say, "It was right to go" or, if they belong to groupings which use more personal language, "The Lord showed us the way". The difficulty with this kind of talk is that any guidance I think I am receiving is filtered or changed by the cultural expectations with which I inadvertently concur. My aspirations become no more than religious rationalization of personal desire.

Those employed by the church are involved too. The ministers of one denomination I know had, for a while, an average length of stay in any one parish of approximately three years. Isn't that *too* short? I remember once an old Scottish professor of theology explaining to a group of students that, earlier in the century, it used to be common practice in Scotland for a minister to stay thirty or forty years in one village. There he gradually learned the people's ways. He became a part of what he ministered to. The professor was laughed at. "No one does that any more." Could it be that now is time for all Christians, whether cleric or lay, to rediscover the calling to stay in one place?

6
Work

Work is a mess! Some people are fighting for more of it—or any at all—while others are agitating for less. Work pleases some, but bores their neighbors. Some live at their work; others rush away from it. We are even confused about what work is. Is it a "job" or more than that? Are "calling" and "work" the same? What will happen to work in Western society?

We are faced with a complex topic. We will therefore examine the biblical teaching in order to obtain a viewpoint from which to proceed, look at "calling" and its relationship to work, notice some facets of work which have gone awry, apply our insights to redundancy (a crucial modern issue) and finally, from all this, reach some conclusions about the place and scope of work for Christian disciples in a confused world.

Work is good but . . .

In the Old Testament, several strands of thought stand out. One of them begins in Genesis where Adam is commanded, while still in the Garden of Eden, to till the soil.[1] That's work. He is also asked to classify the animals God brings to him.[2] That's work too. And both these, physical and mental, are foreshadowed by God's own work, creating the world and people to occupy it.[3]

Then a new element enters with the temptation and the fall, as the Genesis story proceeds:

> [17] *And to Adam he said,*
> *Because you have listened to*
> *the voice of your wife,*
> *and have eaten the tree*
> *of which I commanded you,*
> *"You shall not eat of it"',*
> *cursed is the ground because of you;*
> *in toil you shall eat of it*
> *all the days of your life;*
> [18] *thorns and thistles it shall bring forth to you;*
> *and you shall eat the plants of the field.*
> [19] *In the sweat of your face*
> *you shall eat bread*
> *till you return to the ground,*
> *for out of it you were taken;*
> *you are dust,*
> *and to dust you shall return.*[4]

As a consequence of sin, men and women have to contend with difficulties signified by the thorns and thistles of verse 18 and to endure work as sweaty toil, as explained in verses 19 and 17b. Right here a debate develops. Do these difficulties (toil, the curse on the ground and the expulsion from Eden) mean that work itself is evil? Toil and difficulties enter—about that there can be no dispute—but, although work becomes difficult, the good results from tilling the soil are still possible. Men and women continue to harness the creative processes which God has made. But now they labor to survive, whereas in the world of the Garden of Eden these difficulties were not present. Work has become a *necessary* condition for them to live. As verse 19a shows, work also belongs to that period before humans become dust again. Therefore it has no permanent value, whereas God is eternal. Thus human work is essentially different from God's work. Our work belongs to earthly life. It fades away. Because of the punishment for sin, work is difficult but it is not evil.

From this point on, the Bible narrative assumes that work is an inevitable part of life. For example, Psalm 104 says that man's going forth "to his work and to his labor until the evening" is as natural as the lion hunting and the sun rising.[5] The fourth commandment, which includes the words "Six days you shall labor and do all your work",[6] places work in the category of assumed necessity. So much does work occupy life that one day is to be kept clear of it for worship of the Lord God. No one is free from work. Leaders and kings like David and Noah are described as doing ordinary work[7] and the Bible writers are not in the least embarrassed by this.

But a natural dislike of work is recognized as well. The writer in Proverbs rebukes the sluggard:

> As a door turns on its hinges,
> so does a sluggard on his bed.
> The sluggard buries his hand in the dish;
> it wears him out to bring it back to his
> mouth.[8]

There is no blessing for the lazy loafer. Work has to be done.

Work according to Jesus and Paul

Jesus is assumed to have worked as a carpenter,[9] Paul was a tent-maker[10] and, as such, both were in good rabbinic tradition. The important facts to notice about Jesus' work are first, that if Jesus who was sinless worked, work cannot be evil, and second, that Jesus by working shared one of the most common features of human life. He presumably identified with the toil, difficulty and necessity of work—and also with its rewards. Jesus certainly accepts work and its product as part of life. At the Last Supper[11] for instance, he uses bread and wine, which we today would call products of the food processing industry, in a celebratory feast. This indicates in passing that these work products are at least fitting to be offered as symbols of a most significant event—his own atoning death.

Jesus, as recorded in the Gospels, pays little specific attention to the duties of Christians towards work. But he does speak once or twice of its *distractions*. For example, he rebuked Martha for her over-busyness, by commending Mary's attention to him instead.[12] And work as an excuse for not responding to his call into his kingdom is also condemned—for instance in the parable of the banquet. There one of the guests begged not to come because he had to see a field he had just bought, while another had some oxen.[13]

Although the New Testament writers see work as part of God's ordinance for human beings, they do not treat it as a major theme. Frequently they mention the trade or profession of a particular character, such as Matthew the tax gatherer, Nicodemus a member of the Sanhedrin, the sons of Zebedee who were fishermen, or Lydia the seller of purple.[14] But these are passing references for identification of social status, not for any deeper purpose. When we turn from the Gospels to the rest of the New Testament for reference to everyday work, we find two sets of teaching.

The first is in Paul's writing to the Thessalonians.[15] Paul's teaching was straight from the shoulder and carried a punch, as seen when he wrote to this young and enthusiastic church in Macedonia. Some believers there were preoccupied with the *parousia*, the second coming. Like many discoverers of new spiritual insight, they were over-emphasizing their newfound discovery. They had given up all work and were living off others, while awaiting their Lord's return. Paul would have none of this. "Keep away from any brother who is living in idleness. . . If anyone will not work, let him not eat."[16] There is no doubt that Paul knew that work has to be done.

The second set of teaching is more widely located, but a passage from Colossians expresses the key essentials:

> *Slaves, give entire obedience to your earthly masters, not merely with an outward show of service, to curry favor with men, but with singlemindedness, out of reverence for the Lord. Whatever you are doing, put your whole heart into it, as if you were doing it for the Lord and not for men, knowing that there is a Master who will give you your heritage as a reward for your service. Christ is the Master whose slaves you must be. Dishonesty will be requited, and he has no favorites.*[17]

This passage is frequently appealed to as a basis for how we should regard work in the sense of employment, so it is important to look at it carefully. The "house tables" as they are often called, of which this is one, refer to a particular New Testament situation which no longer exists in the modern Western world. The slave described here is not the criminal slave of the Roman galleys, or the eighteenth century African stolen from his homeland, but a house servant who lived as part of his master's household, enjoying considerable personal esteem and often bearing a great deal of responsibility. To such a house servant the master has, in his turn, a certain responsibility. But privileges or not, the house servant was not free. His master possessed him.

Employers today however are not masters in this master-house servant sense. So no worker need, on the basis of this verse, obey everything a boss says. The boss' area of authority now is job alone, under *agreed* terms. In that sphere an employee must do as asked, but in first century Asia-Minor masters had control over slaves' entire lives.

In assuming that work must be done, the instruction here is in line with all the biblical teaching we have seen so far, but the prime subject of the whole passage[18]—of which our quoted verses are a part—is not work itself. Rather it is the new life with Christ and the consequent relationships between his people, whatever their cultural connections. Thus Paul gives instructions about husbands/wives, parents/children and Christians/outsiders,[19] as well as masters/house servants. The latter instructions therefore only apply to work in the modern factory or office in the most *general* way—namely that Christians are to do everything as if doing it for God. But the instruction applies much more specifically to work done within the relationships of any *family*. We may have replaced human slaves with machines, but cleaning, cooking and caring for children still have to be done. These tasks are to be done well—now by family members—if relationships are to be preserved and enhanced. This passage, then, is teaching Christian families how to live. It is not really about work in the job situation at all.

"That is his lot"

So far we have discussed work in the sense of working for a living—providing what men and women need for food and shelter, and the development of society as a whole. Do we need to say anything more? Are there any specific biblical examples of work being done in a special way to God's glory? There is at least one.

In Exodus 30:30–35 Bezalel and Oholeab are "filled with the spirit of God" to make designs in wood, stone, gold, silver and bronze for the construction of the sanctuary of the ark. But there is no other biblical reference like this. So we cannot build a general doctrine of creativity and inspiration in work on a particular circumstance met by a particular blessing. All we can say is that, in other similar circumstances, God may choose to do the same again.

Do we have to find in work the need to be creative over God's universe? Alan Richardson cautions wisely:

> Some Christian writers have suggested that it is in such creative effort that man primarily displays the image of God in which he was created. But the Bible does not encourage the suggestion that man's work is creative in the same sense as God's.[20]

Or again:

> Admiration of the creative faculty in man may lead to a non-biblical humanism which exalts the creature rather than the Only-Creator. The biblical writers will have none of this (e.g. Psalm 115:4, Isaiah 40:18ff and 49ff, Exodus 32:4 and 1 Kings 12:28).[21]

Work doesn't need to be decorated like a cake with icing. Work is thought by Bible writers to be sweat-producing necessity. The preacher in Ecclesiastes, who is a realist if nothing else, says:

> So I saw that there is nothing better than that a man should enjoy his work, for that is his lot; who can bring him to see what will be after him?[22]

Enjoy it by all means, because it's there! Do it "as to the Lord" as Paul says, because that's what Christians are to do with everything. But there is no mystical or super-spiritual element involved. Work is work—it reeks of the "mannishness of man", and we ought to acknowledge that rather than to try to dodge it.

Useless things

But work is indeed something more, as seen by the God-inspired New Testament writers. They speak a lot about "work" in a distinctive semi-metaphorical sense, to mean working in search of God, or working for and with him both in the church and in the world. For instance after the loaves and fishes incident, Jesus said to the crowds who still looked for him, "Do not labor (work) for the food which perishes but for the food which endures to eternal life". Then the crowd replied, "What must we do to be doing the works of God? to which Jesus rejoined, "This is the work of God, that you believe in him whom he has sent".[23] Man's *belief* in God is God's *work* in man.

In Mark's Gospel there is another example. Jesus commends the woman who honored him by anointing him with precious ointment. He said, "She has done (worked) a beautiful thing (work) to me".[24] "Work" here signifies adoration and worship. Paul uses similar language. For instance in writing against the formation of parties in the local church at Corinth, he says that all Christians are fellow-workers for God and that their work, if they build upon Jesus Christ as foundation, will be rewarded.[25] Later in the same letter he commends Timothy for doing "the work of the Lord".[26]

All these are just a few examples of the main New Testament emphasis. "Work" in this specialized sense is for God and his kingdom. It retains the notion of striving effort, conveyed by words which normally mean hard labor and toil, but it is not what the word "work" usually means. Brede Kristensen, young Danish thinker, deftly catches this dimension by saying:

Ultimate and immediate trust in God is the calling of the Christian. His task is to do "useless" things such as preaching, praying, expressing selfless love and adhering to the wisdom of God—foolishness in the eyes of Greeks and Westerners.[27]

A calling—to what?

Another area of biblical thought often invoked as Christians talk about work is "calling" or "vocation". We commonly express ourselves as being "called to be an accountant, a nurse or a lab technician." When we look at the New Testament where the idea of Christians being called is common, we find there is not even one example of a person being called to a specific job, trade or profession, nor is there any teaching on the subject. However people are called in the New Testament to repentance, to be God's people and to live in fellowship with his Son Jesus Christ.[28] Then they are commanded to be his servants in the work of the church in the world.[29] They are called to "work" in that special, semi-metaphorical sense of work that we have just described.

Richardson speaks correctly when he says:

We must deplore and protest against the secularization of the biblical conception of vocation in our modern usage; we cannot with propriety speak of God's calling a man to be an engineer or a doctor or a schoolmaster. God calls doctors, engineers and schoolmasters to be prophets, evangelists, pastors and teachers as laymen in his church, just as he calls bricklayers, engineers and machine minders.[30]

Those who link work, in the sense of work for a living, with calling frequently appeal to 1 Corinthians 7:20—"Everyone should remain in the state (calling) in which he was called"—assuming that "state" or "calling" means occupation or job. Evidence for that seems slender indeed. None of the other ten New Testament instances of the use of "calling" have that meaning and there seems little reason to introduce it here. This interpretation "has the unanimous testimony of the New Testament against it, for which 'calling' always denotes the call of God's salvation".[31] Paul is asking us to remain in our calling as God's people, whatever our physical or societal state. It is a plea to hold fast to Christian conviction in the world whether one is free, slave or anything else.

Where then does this notion of a Christian's call to work/ occupation come from? It stems from Reformation traditions, for instance in the thought of Martin Luther. He is famous for two illustrations which have become part of our heritage:

> In making shoes, the cobbler serves God, obeys his calling from God, quite as much as the preacher of the Word.[32] God himself will milk the cows through him whose vocation it is![33]

Luther by biblical standards had it wrong. He, and even more those who came after him, extended calling to these areas probably to counter the oppressive elitism of the priestly and monastic orders who saw themselves as "the religious", the only "called ones". They were wrong too, but that doesn't make Luther's extension correct.

Work and calling

So strong is the tradition that work is "calling" and calling "work", that for Christians and many others who have inherited the same work ethic the suggestion that the two are not one causes consternation, both theoretical and practical.

If the two are different, what is the relationship between them?

To help answer that question, let us take as an example Henri Perrin, subject of the extraordinary book *Priest and Worker*, the excruciating yet passionate story of a worker-priest in Germany and France at the end of World War II. He says of those amongst whom he worked:

> . . . *they need a Christian near them, someone who is attractive and doesn't think like everyone else, who behaves in a way that is a witness to the existence of another world where life is happier because people believe in something beyond themselves. I have seen them full of astonishment and admiration when they learned about our prayers, our friendship, our faith. We may not be much in ourselves, but at least they've met Christians, a thing that doesn't happen every day. . .* [34]

Henri Perrin became a workman and went with all his faith, devotion, scholarly understanding and discipline into the work-site at Isere-Arc, a tough workplace by any standards, where fifteen men were killed during the construction of the dam. There he stood for Christ in the midst of noise, labor, argument and cruelly inadequate conditions. The witness was not only personal—though it was certainly that—but was concerned with justice, honor and dignity, fair reciprocal relationships and the taking of action to put right any situation where those qualities were not found.

For Perrin, the daily work was itself at times enjoyable, satisfying, tedious, arduous and exasperating. But always it provided both the financial means to live and a situation in which calling could be exercised. The work environment also provided raw material for a reflection upon how Christians should exercise their calling. Perrin at one point was shocked into thinking about the community of faith:

> *I remember how it hurt me when I asked a Czech
> whether he was a Christian and he said, "What does
> religion matter? We're all workers". When you felt
> the force of the workers' community, what a pitiable
> impression of weakness you get when you speak of
> the Christian community; the thought of the spiritless
> and tired life of practising Catholics hovering around
> their parish priest merely raises a smile. We realize
> all this, but we also realize that the Christian com-
> munity, as it exists at present and is seen by the pa-
> gans   who   surround   us,   is   only   a
> caricature—sometimes only fit to make you weep—of
> the church we really cherish. That's why there is a
> need to create, at least among a few Christians, a
> real Christian community intensely lived in all its de-
> mands—with its faith, passion and power to astonish
> —so that pagans around us will be forced to say:
> "Look how they love one another".[35]*

What Perrin found at work, in this instance a great feeling
of solidarity between people united in a cause, was provocative as he studied, thought and prayed about Christian life.
So work fed calling.

Most of us are not Roman Catholic priests, but the essence
of the Perrin story is applicable to all. The particular work
as such is almost irrelevant. It is a necessity to be done. For
Henri Perrin and for all Christians, work gives one backdrop
of human existence against which Christian calling is lived.

On the theological level, he who disavows the traditional
work/calling identity finds himself faced with charges of
"separating secular and sacred" and having "a non-inte-
grated faith". Certainly Christ is Lord of all. He is center
of the universe[36]—the Bible is clear about that—but his

Lordship will not be complete until our age ends and he comes again. This age is an age of conflict; the kingdom, although here, is not yet fully revealed. The curse of work has not yet been abolished. We are to experience this until we become dust again. Theologically speaking, that's why work is frequently hard, unpalatable and boring for Christians as well as for others. We live in a mixed world of good against evil and evil against good. The redemption which Christ brings does not take us out of this life, or out of the struggle of powers of good vying against powers of evil. It insists we continue to endure here and it gives the power to do so.

The work ethic

The identification of work with calling is one element of what is termed the work ethic. Other typical elements include seeing work no longer as the lot of man, a necessity, but as something which is itself a mark of service to God. Good witness and hard work—even work at the expense of other things—are synonymous.

The story of the development of this ethic through Luther, Calvin, other reformers, the Puritans,[37] the founding fathers of the United States, the early Methodists, nineteenth-century Christian industrialists, the various later Protestant denominations and on into the Catholic workforce—at least in Anglo-Saxon countries—is fascinating. It has been the subject of intensive inquiry. The assertion that it led to the rise of capitalism was offered by Weber and, later, Tawney.[38] Their theses have been attacked and modified by others. But intriguing as such study is, the question for us now is not so much "Where did the work ethic come from?" but rather, given the biblical base we earlier outlined, "How do we put work in its rightful place theologically and practically, as we live as contemporary disciples of Jesus?"

Work gone wrong

Answers to this question will begin to come as we look at some ways in which work, in the tradition of the "work ethic", has gone beyond its place and measure:

1. "Work" has, since the industrial resolution, been more and more identified with "job".

This causes confusion. "Are you working on Saturday?" someone asks and, if you are planning to dig drains at home or rip out a partition in the church hall, you don't know whether to say "Yes" or "No". And those who stay home all week to look after house and children are not usually described as "working"—although they may slave away all day. Indeed I have come to think, after listening to many married women who work in offices and factories, that one of the reasons they take such employment is that staying home is no longer considered socially acceptable because it isn't work!

But then there are strange phenomena on the job scene too. A standby bus driver for instance, waiting for a call, is "working", even though he is actually playing cards— sometimes for hours on end. We should say that he or she is certainly "on the job" at such times, but is not working. Many jobs include payment for non-work time.

We have let "job" almost totally occupy the word "work" —and we should not have done so. Job, occupation, career, trade, profession or whatever one calls it is simply a part of work to be negotiated with an employer or one's customers or clients, to provide a useful function in society and an income on which to live. Work in the ordinary sense, as we have so far seen it in the biblical teaching and examples already referred to, includes *all* that we have to do to sustain ourselves in this world. These biblical examples range over work at home, at a trade, in the market-place, at crafts and in the fields—every area of life of the world of those days.

The Bible writers spoke of work, its character and place in life long before the modern-demarcated "job" came into being. Applying this perspective in today's multi-form society we need to conlcude that whenever effort, either intellectual or physical, is expended to support the life of individual, family, group or country, work is being done. Work, in the ordinary everyday sense, is certainly more than job.

2. People are characterized almost solely by their jobs.

A common first or second question when people meet is, "What are you?" or "What do you do?" and the answer expected is, "I'm a computer programmer", "I'm a lawyer" or whatever. Our job is so important that identity and meaning in life tends to rest there. This frequently leads to disaster if there is no job—through sickness, retirement or unemployment. And quite apart from that possible predicament, do we really want to allow our trades to totally denote us? Are we not people with many gifts, functions and roles quite apart from our jobs?

I might just as legitimately answer the question "What are you?" by saying "I'm a father", and I always feel tempted to reply to the question "What do you do?" by saying "I wander around and pray a bit"—but never have the courage! Moreover it is proper to insist that, for Christians at least, there is life-meaning to be found in being a disciple of Jesus and a member of the church.

3. The virtue accorded to thrift and work leading to

accumulation and retention of wealth has had some bad consequences.

John Wesley is credited with saying, "Gain all you can, save all you can, give all you can". The first two tenets have an uncomfortable habit of overshadowing the third, but even where they don't there is a strong tendency for "rich" to be equated with "good" and "poor" with "bad". This leads to a tough attitude to those who are poor and unemployed, blaming them for being what they are—an atittude which may be truly attributable to some, but which, if held generally, is lamentably uninformed. It ignores the influence of geographic, historical, economic, demographic and political forces, as well as the consequences of more limited educational and familial situations.

4. Work, because it is seen to be so good in itself, is a blinder of conscience.

Several times, agricultural students have been surprised when I have asked them what are their attitudes to productivity on their farms. Would they clear every gully and drain every swamp to increase stock-carrying capacity? Would they fertilize pastures so generously that the streams watering the farm and the one down the valley would choke with accelerated plant growth? And what of the aesthetic? What part does beauty play in farming? Would they give any time, money and effort to making the property look attractive to themselves, their family, their neighbors, their visitors and the next two or three generations? Or is all that besides the point? And what about where their products go? To the rich or poor?

They are usually surprised to be asked such questions and have replied, "We have never thought about these things before." Yet New Zealand is a world leader in many aspects of agriculture and one would think that Christian students here, if nowhere else, would begin to think through such questions. But no, productivity—one of the assumed "goods" of the work ethic—is seldom questioned. The agricultural students and farmers are not alone. Their predicament is shared by many in nearly every area of work in most countries of the Western world. All too few Christians think through the *implications* of the work they do. Work, and especially job, has become so important that it simply overwhelms our sensitivites, our questionings and sometimes our moral scruples. By comparison with the biblical data this viewpoint is quite out of step with a Christian understanding of work.

5. Work has become too important by comparison with individual Christian study, experience and growth.

I am often intrigued that we never bat an eyelid at many years of general and job-orientated education, but expect much less study, practive, tutoring, discipline and experience in spiritual development, except for those "going into the church" or "becoming full-time workers". Isn't it odd that theology, even in the widest sense, is studied by only a few people? If Christian faith is really important to those who are to hold it amid competition from conflicting forces in the work place—or anywhere else for that matter—might not *many* men and women in every local church of every tradition be expected to be as well read in church history, Old and New Testament studies, biblical theology, apologetics and other areas relating Christian faith to today's world as their educational abilities allow? But a lay theologian is still a rarity, often distrusted by those professional in this field and frequently a discomfort to parish ministers.

Is the church then to be full of academic theologians? No,

no! But we need churches full of men and women prepared to limit the time and energy spent in continual traditional work, to give time to Christian study which gives foundation and purpose to Christian activity—men and women willing to let their insight interact with all aspects of life. This is a tremendous need.

It is startling to realize by contrast how much attention Communists give to training of all their people, whatever their educational backgrounds, using a whole variety of methods. Douglas Hyde, author of *Dedication and Leadership*, a comparative study of leadership in Communism and the Christian church, says that while there are a lot of things about Communism which Christians wouldn't want to copy, there are many things from which Christians can learn:

> *This is particularly true of the Communists' attitude to the question of study and formation, and their recognition that those who would serve the cause must establish a unity of theory and practice in their own lives. It is here that the non-Communists tend most often to be at their weakest. It is assuredly where Communists have the greatest strength.*[39]

We need to recover the concept of Christian study as central to vocation.

6. Job takes priority over worship and fellowship.

Quite clearly, the more a person works for an employer, the less time he or she has potentially for life in his or her congregation. More subtly but no less drastically, the rule of job overthrows loyalty to a local church.

Frequently I hear ministers express disappointment as one and then another dependable member of the congregation moves away to a better job, without any consultation, corporate prayer or joint decision-making as to whether or not the move is best for them and their church. Fellowship in the local *ekklesia* often seems to be way down the line of priorities, while "the job" waves its flag gleefully at the top. For a few Christians, job priority may need to be highest at some God-given time in their lives but, even if this should be so for some, it is unlikely to be the case for all, all the time, if the biblical emphasis of work as necessity but not calling is accepted.

7. Preoccupation with work, particularly with "job", leads to a mind-set which evaluates "all else" by work and its characteristics.

This mind-set plays havoc in corporate Christian life, because it is "brought across" into the church by leaders who are usually professional or businessmen. It is a way of looking at things which sees activity and productivity as the measure of successful progress. Allowing this mind-set to unwittingly determine decisions, structures and goals results in the church becoming a hive of activity (just like the rest of society) and of progress being measured, say in an annual report, in terms of statistics of things done.

But the church first and foremost is a *fellowship* in which to live, and not merely an institution in which to work or a building to attend. The sociological entities in which we find our true meaning as persons and our vocations as Christians have to be measured very differently from the way in which we measure the function of an institution or the productivity of a business.

8. The work ethic, if over-emphasized, brings a preoccupation with work for its own sake.

Family, spouse, friend "go to the wall" for the sake of work. In surprisingly large numbers the result is the workaholic. Udo Middleman illustrates predicament of the workaholic by citing an example from his experience at L'Abri in Switzerland, a place of refuge for many wanting to sort out meaning in life:

> *I remember a man who came to us some time ago. His wife had accused him of having an engineer's syndrome; all he did was think engineering and play with figures. She wanted to divorce him and we can feel for her. For the engineer had not managed to control his environment, and his environment had shaped him.*[40]

There are student study syndromes, teachers', accountants', social workers', housewives', mechanics', factory supervisors' and farmers' syndromes—plus a thousand others! Tragically, many of us don't realize what is happening. We actually admire it. Peter Wagner gets near the heart of the matter in a personal, provocative little thinkpiece when he says:

> *Work becomes a vice. It is pure and simple an escape mechanism from the anxieties of life. Work can be escape from family tensions. It can be a device to overcome inferiority complexes. It can, in its final stage, become an escape from oneself and even from God. When it does, let's call it what it is—a sin! The reason why workaholism is a more difficult sin to deal with than alcoholism is that society reinforces it rather than condemns it. The Protestant ethic makes the hard worker the paradigm of virtue and even comes up with biblical and theological justification for it. Work is so respectable that some will have a very difficult time in accepting the thesis of this essay, namely that it can become a vice.*[41]

Not all of us are at the extremes of work addition described by Middleman and Wagner, but many—gloriously unaware —are zooming up the graph on the way to becoming so.

9. Choosing a job has become too important.

This is largely because work has been thought of as a calling and because "work" and "job" have become synonymous. These points we have already discussed. I often wonder why we lose so much sleep over "What will I be?" where the expected answer is farmer, scientist or shop assistant. It's the wrong question, but the wrong answer. I will be a disciple and servant of my Lord! Does it matter in what occupation? Shouldn't I just seek one to fit my talents, interests, experience, monetary needs, availability and qualifications?

Christians often seem to have more difficulty than non-Christians in choosing jobs, and yet Christians say they are guided. The search and the decision for the right job has been made too special, too esoteric, too vital. We ought to be more relaxed about such matters, particularly as we have a vocation separate from our routine job.

Good things about the work ethic

Faced with this depressing catalogue, we must quickly reverse the coin and acknowledge that *good* things have come from the modern emphasis on work. The right of all to work for a fair wage finds support in biblical teaching that work is the lot of man and that the laborer is worthy of his hire.[42] Fair treatment of workers by the boss finds antecedent in Paul's teaching about how a master should treat slaves.[43] And without the idea that work is important and necessary, much useful human achievement and cultural stability of the last two or three centureis would not have taken place.

But work has run away with itself. In this chapter we have been trying to hold it back, first by examining its biblical base and secondly, by pointing out some of its run-away consequences. Now, in order to continue to put it in its right place for contemporary disciples, we must address the question of shrinking job numbers.

A Crucial modern issue: redundancy

We need first to focus on the electronic or information revolution[44] as it affects work. It will bring huge change, a first symptom of which will be structural unemployment. For instance, the changes "could mean that of eighteen to nineteen million typists and secretaries in Western Europe, five million could lose their jobs in the next ten years", according to a report compiled in 1978.[45] As memory typewriters, word processors, printouts and computer filing quickly take over, the clerical-secretarial area of employment will be one of the first and hardest hit. A 1978 report in France estimated that 30% of the jobs in banking and insurance (most of which are of a secretarial-clerical nature) could disappear over the next decade.[46] No country in the Western world is immune from it. All are following each other. Nor will other industires stand aside. Automatic warehouses, electronic funds transfer, automated assembly lines[47] and one thousand other innovations will take away huge numbers of jobs.

Some new employment will be created, especially in the micro-electronics field itself. Then there may be expansion in industries developing "software" (i.e. programs) for the new equipment. There will also be some employment gains in new and redesigned industries based on micro-electronics, making cheap consumer goods—such as watches and TV games—for home and commercial use. But no one knows how much employment all these innovations will provide. All we can predict is that htese new industries themselves will be highly automated.[48]

The effect of the information revolution in creating unemployment is compounded by demographic trends. As the 1980s unfold, the "baby boom" will still be hitting the workplace, bringing many more men and women to seek jobs. Whereas in the Depression and slumps of the earlier twentieth century the unemployed were largely adult men, now they are gratudates of both sexes. They have been educated for jobs, at least in a general way, but there are not enough available.

Not everyone agrees with these predictions. Employers tend to make lower unemployment estimates than unions. A wide range of people in all walks of life dismiss these ideas as either fantasy or gloom. Others who do acknowledge the reality have a basic optimism that, in some unforeseen way, there will be thousands of new jobs, although they admit that some present ones will disappear. Proponents of this view remind us that the industrial revolution in its many facets of development provided diverse and increasing employment opportunities. It's a piety they gloss over both the agony of the social upheaval at the time and the fact that the new revolution will affect a larger population still living in the same land area, a population much more related to each other in economic necessity than one hundred years ago.

Time will tell who is right—no serious predictor would claim infallibility—but I fail to see how we can ignore the reality of widespread unemployment and disruption for a considerable period. There is too much evidence now, both actual and indicative.

A future scenario

Let us imagine what might happen if we put the future and our redescribed idea of work together. Farming, industry, trade and all the associated services will variously require fewer and fewer hours of traditional work. At first this will be very unequally distributed, because those who have jobs will hold on grimly to them. There will be lots of discussion and dispute, but eventually traditional defensive positions held by groups such as the trade unions will be abandoned and job hours as we now understand them will be redistributed—fewer among more. Thus shorter days, weeks, years and lifetimes in traditional jobs will be worked, and there will be frequent periods of retraining to accommodate change, both to new industries and to new methods in old industries. At the same time the general public, government and pressure groups such as employer associations will gradually, if reluctantly, recognize that work is more than traditional job. Take some examples.

I might, with other local people, keep a river on the outskirts of the town where I live discriminately free from willow trees and from litter, to preserve it for swimming, boating, fishing and picknicking. Or I may spend a lot of time in a neighborhood craft cluster. Alternatively I might be involved in some aspect of people care—geriatric for instance—under the auspices of my church, not just through institutions but by visiting and helping in people's homes. I might even stay at home to look after children, which would include working with them in some aspects of local school life. These sorts of activities, which I previously crushed into spare time, will be done for a substantial number of hours per week. They are all *work*. And how will I be paid?

From the government I will receive my share of the wealth earned by farming, industry and trade. I'll need to be paid not only that I might survive or because any work deserves reward, but because industry needs my buying power. Consumption of goods and services is essential to industry's existence, so industry must share its profits in order to perpetuate itself. It used to do so by wages and dividends; in the future it will have to do so by allowing its wealth to be taken and redistributed.

Inane, ludicrous, innovative nonsense? It may seem so, but I do not think it is. Sooner or later some version, partial or otherwise, of this scenario will come—unless incompetent chaos or totalitarian autocracy prevails. If sooner, it will be because Christians, with others, take a lead in bringing it about. If later, it will be after very bitter struggle as we stubbornly insist on trying to retain the status quo.

I remember a course I attended to which representatives from political parties, workers, employers, promotional and planning groups were invited, to discuss with us their vision of industry in the next twenty years. All made approximately the same diagnoses about large-scale change and unemployment and nearly all made the same recommendation: fight somehow (though it was not clear how) to keep what we have and get more out of it. There seemed little realization of, and planning for, the consequences of the new trends. What a pity! We will need to grapple with these implications—and quickly too!

Christian responsibility

I do not mean that we should simply accept all change as it comes. We do not want to wake up one morning and find that the previous day's scene has changed overnight as though an ubiquitous revolving stage had quietly turned around. To some proposed changes both in work and beyond it we will need to say, "No!" This we have already discussed in our chapter on means and ends.[49] We don't want to be swamped by technical means. There is a need to see consequences and be sure that the change envisaged is of long-term benefit. Sin will exhibit itself in the future much as it does now. We are not talking about a coming utopia, but we are looking at massive change.

As these changes arrive, stride by giant stride, any work place will become a forum for discussion. Christians are in all these places alongside everyone else. There is a Christian lead to be given, a Christian responsibility to be exercised. But I worry that many of us, content to believe that living for God is purely a personal matter, will just go along with whatever changes happen, without giving other possibilities serious scrutiny. I worry also that many Christians will *join* those who fight for an uncritical retention of our present way of life. It's only posturing to fight for that which is impossible to attain. Moreover such a demand is also basically designed to retain the same style and standard of living as that which prevails now. And we have already seen that such a style is of doubtful tenure for Christians. We need to return to our discussion of work and calling. Can we doubt that our French worker-priest was following his calling to be his Lord's disciple and servant? He, like Jesus before him, went where the people were, and he followed through with positive action which stemmed from his convictions. In our technological society, as compared with his industrial one, we have to do the same.

We will start in a position of strength if we have wrestled with the biblical teaching on work and come to some understanding of it. Christians are to know that their first task is always "work" in that other sense of "the work of the Lord," the so-called unless things of expressing selfless love and adhering to the wisdom of God. So Christians are not to be captivated by daily work for its own sake, even when work, rightly understood, is more than a job. They are therefore in a strong position in times of great social change to stand in any work place, but yet aside from it, and give a lead in ensuring that justice, with other qualities which flow from God, are upheld.

Christians, like it or not, are by Paul's words "the leaven in the lump."[50] This means they must protect fellow men and women, whether Christian or not, from being engulfed by technical achievement or materialistic gain. In doing so they will be showing love and declaring truth. And Christians can't do any work "as to the Lord" without asking about the *rightness* of that work. Consequently Christians will often be unpredictable. They won't be the unequivocable champions of the unions, the bosses, a political party or any pressure group. They will speak truth where they find it and may be interpreted sometimes as changing sides. They may agitate against one change towards the information or automated society, but for another.[51] Yet they will constantly fight against greed for wealth and greed for power,[52] at any level in the coming turmoil.

Where Christians themselves are powerless or overruled, they are called to be loving and long-suffering as the house servants of overbearing masters were encouraged to be:

> . . . if when you do right and suffer for it you take it patiently, you have God's approval. For to this you have been called, because Christ also suffered for you, leaving you an example, that you should follow in his steps.[53]

And always, as we saw in our first chapter, Christians are to be conscious that they are in the time of Christ,[54] a time of invitation to people to believe in him. In periods of great social disorientation, men and women will need more than ever before to be shown where meaning in life lies. And ultimately that means introduction to Jesus Christ as the giver of new life, through his death and resurrection.

A knife edge

Our survey of work has cast up many areas needing care and caution, but also areas lying waiting for imaginative initiative and innovation. Christians have to walk a knife edge in regard to work. Work is good, yes. The right to work for all is to be defended, provided work is widely understood—and not equated with job. Work is not all important. It is not to dictate the scene. It's not a calling, yet it is essential to the existence of human society. Work, as part of the mannishness of man, has no permanent or eternal qualities. Work, whether at home, in a neighborhood project or in ordinary jobs, is one of the environments of life in which a Christian is to live in the kingdom in the world.

But the greatest importance rests with that other sort of "work"—work in that special New Testament sense of the search and service for God. And *that* work is always available to all, everywhere.

7
Leisure

The meaning of "work" has, as we saw in the last chapter, to be enlarged to include many activities we have not usually branded with that name. Yet we have also seen that work, especially job, can consume us.

A lady I know grew up as a daughter of a nursery-man. If ever she was seen reading a book, she was heavily castigated and told to "get outside and weed the roses." The family lived at work and for work; relaxation such as reading for pleasure was a waste of time. Yet we could eavesdrop in households where the common complaint is that some or all are always out, surfing, at meetings, at bingo or somewhere else. Too much leisure—or not enough? What is leisure anyway.

Although some people want to work all the time, most of us view work as "have to" and leisure as "want to." Leisure is "time at our own disposal"—to quote one denominational declaration about the Christian use of leisure.[1] That is probably the definition that the majority of us accept. Within this prescription we can fit voluntary study, visiting, sport, hobbies, television viewing, arts, crafts, worship and a host of other pastimes—including sitting in the sun!

Just as work is one backdrop of life against which disciples are to live,[2] leisure is another. Just as with work there are situations into which Christ's love or truth (or both) have to be taken and spoken, so there are with leisure. Therefore some debate about the issues involved is necessary if we are not to be sucked holus-bolus into whatever prevails at any one time. What is leisure's place and importance? What are leisure's characteristics to be? What insights do Christian perspectives give? This chapter tries to answer these questions.

Leisure: are we on the right track?

Samuel Kamaleson of World Vision once said that one of the main problems in our world is that too often we give material answers to spiritual questions.[3] That's what we frequently do in the field of leisure. Leisure time is supposedly when we enjoy ourselves either immediately or as the result of something else. It has to do with how we feel in relation to people, animals, things, ideas and God—all of which give life meaning.

Enjoyment in leisure is therefore a spiritual matter. All sorts of things can be used as the "props" for attaining that enjoyment. Food, books, games, beautiful drapes, outings, drinks at the bar—a whole plethora of alternatives wait to be used. But with the bursting out of affluence in the last few decades, the props have changed roles. We are, writes Gordon Dahl, possessed by a "virtuous materialism":

> There is some basis for arguing that our society is investing more of its resources, human and natural, in the consumption of material goods than in their production. For example, traditional economics measures the cost of say a snowmobile in terms of the investment made to produce it. But of what value is a snowmobile that is never used? And what man having paid a price for it will not attempt to get his money's worth by using it as much as he can? But

using a snowmobile (or any other so-called leisure goods) takes time. It may take some of a man's work time, but more likely it will cut into his non-work time—i.e. his "free" time. Obviously, therefore, the more leisure goods a man acquires, the more time and energy he will commit to using them and the less truly free time he will have left.[4]

Those of us who do not live in North America might smile at the snowmobile illustration but, as Dahl himself suggests, couldn't the lesson apply to a whole range of bits and pieces from cloths to vacation homes, from fishing rods to automobiles? There is a strong tendency for the props to become the central characters. A spiritual issue—finding satisfying leisure—is often being given a material solution.

Related to this cluttering of pleasure chattels is the preference people have for money rather than time. Writing of the situation historically in Great Britain, David Bridge says:

Increases in real wealth can be taken in various ways, but are mainly taken either as extra income or as extra leisure. Though our society has shown a general preference for greater income, the degree of preference has not always been the same. From 1840 to 1870 the proportion in which increased wealth was taken as income as against leisure was 59:41. From 1870 to 1905 it rose to 78:22. It fell during the period 1905–1930 to 61:39, due to statutory reduction of working hours which followed the First World War and also to the general economic recession toward the end of that period. Since then, up to 1953, the proportion has risen to 80:20. So the overall picture is of a growing preference for more income as against more leisure since the middle of last century.[5]

And the money, it would seem, is used to buy leisure things.

Walter Kerr, in *The Decline of Pleasure*, puts his finger on another aspect of how leisure time freedom has changed:

> *We are all of us compelled to read for profit, party for contacts, lunch for contracts, bowl for unity, drive for mileage, gamble for charity, go out for the evening for the greater glory of the municipality, and stay home for the weekend to rebuild the house.*[6] *And if that list sounds "middle-class" or middle-age, the addition of "collect bottles for the gang, solicit for the returned soldiers, demolish a house to raise funds for the football club and disco for the starving in Asia" extends the point to most education and age-groups. Leisure, supposedly "free," has all of a sudden become a chore. It has taken on many of the characteristics of work.*

Leisure seems further "mixed-up" by two seemingly contradictory trends, which in fact reinforce each other. One is leisure over-choice and the other is watching TV. The first is highlighted by the title of a book by Staffan B. Linder, *The Harried Leisure Class*.[7] In any town or city in any of our "developed countries" a huge range of hobbies, amusements, sports and recreations is available. Football on Saturday and church on Sunday has long since disappeared. Think of anything and someone plays it. Name it and someone collects it. Invent a new feat of prowess and you'll find a world mark for it already in the *Guinness Book of Records*. We are harried by the choice available. Yet television keeps people at home, isolated (alone or with partner), watching others living, doing, playing, making or collecting. This huge variety of recreational activity is suddenly vicariously there for all. By doing it second-hand we can "do" even more, and so leisure time becomes as crowded as a

Tokyo train where pushers stand to propel people in.

We have described some areas of life where leisure has misfired—misfired to the point of denying one of its key components, freedom. If Christians are to function meaningfully within their leisure time, they need to find a Christian base from which to work and it is therefore to a consideration of these biblical components we now turn.

A Christian view of leisure

Although we will be deeply frustrated if we search for a biblical doctrine of leisure to be applied like some set formula, there are a number of biblical elements that are clearly applicable:

(a) Rejoicing

John the Baptist's disciples must have been either very glum or very earnest, because by contrast Jesus' men and women were accused of being a jovial lot. Jesus was rebuked because his disciples behaved as if they were having a continual celebration. Fasting, prayer and the call for repentance had a very important place in Jesus' life and teaching, but when answering the criticism of his disciples' way of life he said, "Can the wedding guests fast while the bride-groom is with them? As long as they have the bride-groom with them, they cannot fast."[8]

For disciples, to be with Jesus was then, and is now, an occasion of great joy. We have already seen[9] how important joy and celebration are in the Christian's life. Parties, feasts, holidays, music and relaxation together are all expressions of the life of joy. They are some of the ingredients of leisure.

(b) Sunday

Old Testament teaching closely sets aside one day in seven

to be given to non-work, when Yahweh can be expecially worshipped.[10] But the new covenant wipes away the old; law is replaced with freedom and grace. It is not surprising therefore that Jesus stood firmly against the sabbath as it was currently practiced and taught by Jewish leaders. He seems to have made a point of healing on that day[11] to underscore the fact that God's goodness and holiness could be appropriately dispensed then, and that prohibition of healing on the seventh day was a zealous legalistic mistake. Most famously he taught that:

> The sabbath was made for man, not man for the sabbath; so the Son of Man [Jesus] is Lord even of the Sabbath.[12]

This gives to his followers an enormous liberty. Jesus did not abolish the keeping of one day in seven as different and worshipful. But he did *free* it from fierce rigidity. For instance, the New Testament never transfers to the Lord's day the specific regulations regarding sabbath rest. Jesus says the sabbath is made for man to use, but that he himself is its Lord. Therefore very suitably it became, as the early church lived on, a feast day to celebrate the resurrection. It was commemorated on the first day of the week[13] because that was the day of resurrection[14] and also the day of Jesus' first appearance to his disciples after the crucifixion.[15] This new sabbath picks up the life of joy and focuses it on one day. It is a time when the risen Lord and his people gather together. The salvation brought by Jesus' death and resurrection is celebrated in worship, and this celebration becomes also an announcement to the world at large of what he has done.

Sunday asks that Christians worship together in their congregations. Detailed discussion of forms service is irrelevant —to our discussion at least. To allow expression of joy—

along with the other qualities of awe, reverence and thankfulness—is the essence of the new covenant, Lord's day celebration. The joy is to be expressed, not just felt individually, so that Christians together can recognize and share what Jesus has done for them. If worship allows that joy to be expressed and responded to, it is appropriate worship; if it doesn't, then it needs to change. No stultifying form, whether it be liturgical or conventionally unstructured, is to curb the expression of the people of God rejoicing together.

But having agreed that joyous celebration of the people together is to be a feature of Sunday, what else is in harmony with Jesus's teaching that the sabbath is made for man and Jesus himself is its Lord? A minor tragedy of church history is that Sunday observance has been a matter of dispute. A more major tragedy is that for some groups it has been, and sometimes still is, a day of strict repression. To make Sunday a day of regulation is to return it to the legalism from which it was rescued by Jesus. If there is any day on which leisure is best exercised it is Sunday, provided that what is done fits with what the day is for. Leisure is freedom and freedom comes in Christ. Sunday celebrates Christ's freeing man from sin by death and resurrection, and therefore freedom ought to characterize Sunday life: Sunday carries with it the Old Testament concept of a pause from work, so work (as we have understood it in the last chapter) ought to be absent from Sunday as much as possible—provided that we do not lurch backwards into a pool of legalism. I heard of a family that switched all their lights on before going to bed on Saturday night and left them on all next day, to avoid the work of turning them on when Sunday dusk arrived! Surely they were in danger of *drowning* in that pool!

Essential services, such as hospital care and food production, are matched by Jesus' healing on the Sabbath and his

disciples picking corn to eat.[16] Instances like that should
therefore dispel pointless argument about the rights and
wrongs of Sunday work in these areas of life. But if work
is being done simply to grow rich, heighten productivity
against competitors or make living more luxurious, Christians should opt out or, better, try to change their employment hours and even the operating times of the businesses
in which they work. That may involve quite deep debate
with one's work colleagues and employers. In my experience, however, a lot of workers and their living partners will
be grateful for Christians taking a lead to ensure that at least
one day in seven is kept completely free. Continual work,
even if wealth producing, is exhausting!

But the biggest danger for Christians and others is that
the day can become so materialist and "thing" orientated,
that pause from work disappears in a sea of leisure activity
which exhausts as much as any regular work. The cars, the
canned foods, the sports gear, vacation wear, outdoor and
camping equipment and a million other things must be "consumed" so that more can be sold—a point already taken from
Gordon Dahl.

And when will consumption occur? Why, on Sunday.
Saturday is frequently either busy with work or not long
enough for all the planned "free time" activities. So Sunday
is the great leisure-goods user. Before we know it Sunday
has become, particularly for the younger age-group, a day
of whirlwind travel and consumption. For many, freedom,
the essence of leisure, disappears in the false expectations
generated by compulsive consumerism and mass advertising. For Christians specifically the attitude of joyful celebration, if attained by worship together, is lost in the "before
and after" conformity to the same consumptive rush—a rush
compounded by the activity emphasis of church life (meetings, etc.), generated in its turn by the work-based mind-set

which is so prevalent in church leadership.

Christian individuals, families, communities and churches can still make choices about what fills Sunday. How will they choose? I hope they will keep freedom, joy, worship and people as criteria of choice. Moreover it seems vitally necessary for Christians to help each other make the most of Sunday, refusing to settle for something either dreary and dull or brittle and hurried. The brightest clothes, appealing but simple food, cheerful books, favorite games, easiest-to-relax-with friends and, if possible, some enjoyment of God's created world all seem fitting.

(c) Care

Congregational, Sunday rejoicing spills over into fellowship together, which in turn leads to concern and care for each other. If ever we are tempted to minimize the place of leisure, we need to remember that leisure porvides time in which to care. If there is too much work, caring is ignored; the productivity chase drives concern for other people away. It is true that Christian care given in leisure time may become work, as in the example of the care of elderly people. Indeed we enlarged the meaning of work to include just such activities. Any real care always has a work component, because strict demarcation is not a natural characteristic of life. Work and leisure intermingle. Arguing about whether taking someone to the doctor or drinking coffee with them at home is work or leisure is unprofitable.

Being together has many elements. Some care starts as leisure choice, then becomes moral obligation accompanied by strenuous effort; some care travels the reverse path. Here too, there enters that other sort of "work," that giving oneself to search for and serve God which we saw to be more important to New Testament writers than work as we normally speak of it. "Work" in that special sense is the Christian's calling and can be exercised in leisure just as it can in any other aspect of life.[18] If leisure is time at our own disposal, we will spend some of it in deliberate care for others. But if caring activity becomes for any individual, group or family the *only* characteristic of leisure, then something has gone wrong. Leisure will have become work again.

(d) Talents

Another appropriate part of leisure is using our given and developed human talents. They are used in work too, but in leisure they frequently have more untrammelled scope. Whether Joe paints and Sally visits, Bill fishes or Nola reads is really beside the point. What is important is that God-given abilities are used for oneself and others. Therefore one expects crafts, hobbies, sports and many other kinds of pleasurable pastimes to be pursued by Christians, provided that our previous points about pleasure goods, work-characterized leisure time and the danger of giving human creations too much status are given serious consideration as leisure activities are chosen and enjoyed.

Nor should the exercise of individual talent be seen as a licence for selfishness. The trumpet player who throws a party may not find time and place easy to locate! Leisure can also be a force for selfish evil in another way, namely when it carries with it an uncaring attitude to the created world. We so easily rip, pull, chop, hurt, destroy, litter, poison and soil in the name of enjoying ourselves. This was underlined for me in a trivial but important way when I was at a cricket match with an older friend, whom I had come to respect for the love he showed to other people. After lunch he threw his food discards on the ground. I'm sure he didn't deliberately say to himself, "OK, the world's a rubbish dump—here I go!" Everybody else was littering—it took days for the organizers to clean the grounds—and without thinking, so entrapped in consumer ways was he, he just conformed.

Christians at leisure need to conserve rather than consume, to preserve rather than pollute. Indeed we can be even more positive. Creativity, even though it crumbles to dust and is not to be a monument to perpetuity, can produce a little space of beatuy, peace, laughter or satisfaction around us which is, for a shorter or longer time, both relaxing and enriching.

In the use of talents in leisure activity there is another battle to be fought. There is a fine distinction between spurring each other on and competing aggressively. Winning can become so important that hate and jealousy arise rather than relaxation and fun. Christians should be motivated to love and serve. That motivation is incapatible with many of the "win at all costs" commercial and nationalistic elements in modern competition. In these areas Christians have an important contribution to make in sportsmanship. I like the comment of Daniel Thomas Jenkins in his book *Christian Maturity and the Theology of Success:*

> Some highly successful and no less highly rewarded professionals in sport make an open confession of their piety and say it helps their performance. Their witness would be more impressive if it led them sometimes to take light-hearted and expensive risks, just for fun, to underline the fact that all this is only a form of play.[19]

Surely that remark is apposite to all sport and Christian witness in it. Some accepted ways in sport need to be protested. For instance, warlike "psyche-up" pep talks by coaches ("I want you to go out there and take them apart—kill them.") can't go unnoticed by Christian team members. And if the coach won't change, that team may have to be deserted for another.

(e) Rest

One element has remained outside our discussions so far: rest. A famous verse which has passed into our culture, not only because millions of Anglicans and Episcopalians have heard it every communion service but because it speaks to the very center of anxious man, is:

> *Come to me, all who labor and are heavy laden and I will give you rest.* [20]

Rest means "refreshment." It is freedom from anxiety, worry, oppression and heavy toil. The word "labor" is the same one which Peter used when he said, after that heavy night of fishing, "Master, we have *toiled* all night and caught nothing."[21] So it is a word meaning very exhausting effort. And Jesus continued:

> *Take my yoke upon you, and learn from me; for I am gentle and lowly in heart and you will find rest for your souls. For my yoke is easy and my burden is light.* [22]

This comment was directed towards those in Judaism overconscious of the demands of pernickety law. Trying to keep such a law could be a labor indeed. Today the majority of citizens do not live under a vigorously interpreted Mosaic code, but many others labor in much the same way under severe cultural expectations—usually "get more and spend more"—that have the same constricting effect. Freedom from all that is offered in Christ. Here is an invitation to permanent rest (in the sense that we have just seen) by becoming a follower of Jesus. It looks forward to the permanent rest which comes on the other side of death. It is the beginning now of a two-way relationship with God which goes on forever.

But because it is a permanent relationship which depends upon carrying out the command "learn from me," its continuance demands special drawing aside to be with the resurrected Jesus. This "drawing aside" fits best in leisure time when people are comparatively free of external restraints. Jesus is here not talking about sabbath observance of fellowship togehter. He is underscoring the quality and result of a personal relationship with him.

We saw earlier that one of the characteristics of the Christian life is "with God" privacy.[23] This is withdrawal from the activity of daily work to be alone with God. As Christians take their leisure, being with God to maintain a permanent "gentle yoke" would seem to be a top candidate for time. Yet as I listen to many Christian people, I fear that the crush of daily life continually squeezes out private time with God. Leisure so often takes on the characteristic of work. It is all bustle, push and responsibility. It is regulated into segments of measured time just like work; it is stolen for work to maintain or obtain more things. So leisure time with the Master disappears.

I long to see a widespread surge of enthusiasm to be with God. The Catholic tradition preserves the routine of daily office—in obedience if not always in joy; the evangelical tradition preserves the disciplined personal "quiet time"—in exhortation if not in fact; and the newer charismatic mood picks up with noisy enthusiasm elements of repetitional praise such as "Thank you Lord, thank Lord, thank . . . " But none of these traditions quite grasps the "with God" privacy, which was so much part of the rhythm of life Jesus lived with his disciples.

In leisure today people use their imaginations. All kinds of activities proliferate, but in finding time to be with God Christians at leisure seem strangely dull. There are some who show us the way. A returned missionary I knew used to walk at the waves edge of a surf beach, shouting and laughing with his Lord. A former colleague, returning home after a trip away, would go for two days to a little cabin in a vineyard and talk himself out to God—telling him the agony and joys of his travelling ministry until he was exhausted. Then sleep would take over for many hours before he returned to his wife, family and the hustle-bustle of ordinary life. An older friend from time to time would take a free-flowing modern translation of the New Testament from his shelf, sit down in a comfy chair and read a whole Gospel straight through, to reflect upon and feel the impact of the total message.

The opportunities to be with God in a more-particular-than-usual relationship are limitless and, within these imaginative moments, can come all the classic prayer modes of Christian history: confession, praise, meditation, thanks, petition and intercession. They need not be passed by. In whatever ways are appropriate, including periodic retreat perhaps, there is a great need to live imaginatively—to find the time and rhythm of being with people, but alone with God.

But there is another point. We have seen that work often passes on its characteristics to leisure. Is there any scope for *leisure's* restful freedom to be transferred to work? Of course any factory supervisor will recount with vengeful relish tales of workers who have been only too keen to bring leisure to work. That's not what we're talking about! Laziness on the job is not a Christian goal. But a Christian restfulness, cultivated in leisure, is invaluable in the tension, pressure and sometimes panic of daily work. The Christian worker who draws on his rich experience of leisure time with God may show joy, peace, gentleness, kindness and other God-given traits. He or she can become a respected, stable influence in school or office, on the shop floor and in the home, neighborhood or wherever else work is done.

There is another way in which the life of prayer cultivated in leisure can spill over directly into the remainder of life, particularly work. A quarrel observed can result in interior prayer[24] for peace there and then. Over-authoritarian display by a boss can turn us, almost in conditioned response, to prayer for the man's freedom from egotism and pressure. A tension headache bemoaned by a friend calls for interior intercession for his or her relief from anxiety. This ability as a matter of automatic response, to pray in the quiet of one's mind to our great transcendent God about all the incidents of life, is greatly needed today. How I wish that a Christian revolution of this sort—prayer in every circumstance, taking its roots in leisure time spent with God— would send branches and shoots into all parts of society where Christians go.

Leisure is good

We have gathered together a Christian view of leisure that is essentially practical, stemming from biblical teaching about rejoicing and celebration, the character of Sunday, care for each other, the use of natural talents and the significance of rest. In addition, we will become aware that many of our other topics have their own impact upon leisure. Thus our determination not to be swamped by *technical means* affects leisure, in that decisions have to be made about how technically complex or perfect our recreation equipment and arrangements will be. If we take seriously the journey to *simplicity*, we have some guidelines regarding the purchase of leisure goods in days when many people in the world are starving. *Mobility* raises questions too. If we are intent upon being a called people in a chosen place, high-level pleasure mobility either around the world or even in one's own country scarcely fits. Then *privacy* needs consideration. An individual can spend masses of time alone in amusement or reverie, to the detriment of the communal aspect of Christian life. Yet, as we have seen, solitude with God is important.

And *time* and leisure? In a very real sense the definition of leisure as "time at our own disposal" is simply not accurate. For Christians, all time is God's; no time is ours to do what we like with. But there are "times of leisure" given to us in trust. And it is exciting to know that, if we are willing to declare that leisure is good and has an important place in life, then God will help us find and preserve those times.

8
The car

A SYMBOLIC CASE STUDY

I come from a land of wheels. At the last count New Zealand had one car for every 2.6 people![1] But the summer I spent in Austria staggered me. I hadn't realized what people meant when they talked about "Europe on holiday." The road past the castle in which I spent five weeks was a scenic link to Italy. The traffic density for twelve or fifteen hours a day was so intense that sometimes I had to wait ten minutes on the roadside before scurrying across—and this was in the country! Big cars and little cars, all decorated with bundles of holiday equipment, passed by in endless procession, drawn on by some giant holiday magnet located somewhere near the Mediterranean.

When I first went to India, I was emotionally over-whelmed by the vast numbers of people sitting everywhere: on all the corners, on steps, along the roads, under trees and on railway platforms. No place was empty of human beings. In Europe I didn't notice people—I saw only cars.

Wheels, wheels, wheels

The trip to work, the weekly pick-up of groceries, the week-end family outing, the pleasant drive to the neighborhood golf course, the hectic chase after the best surf, the dry ride on a wet day from the garage at home to the parking lot at church, the routine collection of Mother from the old folks' home to bring her to Sunday dinner—all these conveniences, and many others, are made possible by the car. It has been a great facilitator and time-saver. It is especially a facilitator of *choice*. With it I choose my shop, my hairdresser, my child's ballet teacher, my friends and a hundred and one commercial, public or pleasurable services.

It is difficult for those who live in the technocratic market economies to imagine life without private cars. Cars have been embraced by all. If we do not own a car, we aspire to do so. We save desperately to become car owners and, once we are, we enjoy buying a new model, even if it is only "new" to us, every few years.

As we gaze upon our vehicle, together with its thousands of fellows standing stationary in a rush-hour snarl, we realize that, because of its sheer numbers, the private car is probably a fitting symbol of Western society. It stands for independence, freedom and the right to move! Yet over it, both for what it has done and for what it will do in the future, there hang some questions—questions for everybody.

Christians concerned about how to live for Christ in this world have a particular responsibility to consider the issues raised. As well as transporting, the car kills, pollutes, eats land, swallows energy, helps break up families, promotes facile relationships, encourages aggression, extends violence and provides delusions of grandeur. And yet Christians have joined the great car excursion as much as anybody. Yes, certainly there are questions to be asked and answered!

A multi-method polluting agent

Rene Dubos and Barbara Ward, well-known thinkers about

man in his environment, note that cars (among which private cars are far the most numerous) are our second most serious air polluter.[2] Stand on any busy city corner and evidence of this is abundant. Country areas have exhaust gas pollution of another sort. New Zealand research has shown a large lead build-up in roadside grasses as driving has increased, to the point where grazing of the parkway, or even of field pasture close to the road, is thought unwise because of the consequent contamination of animals which may be used for meat.[3]

Litter alongside roads, on river banks, in parks and rest places shows what happens when peoples become privately mobile. Suddenly, sheer mobility makes the population seem larger and dirtier than it is. The automobile allows the spreading fingers of rubbish pollution to stretch further out, far beyond the residences from where it comes.

Private mobility pollution does not stop at roadsides. Because people in huge numbers now go to places of great scenic attraction, they have to do something when they get there. So they hike, fish, canoe, ride horses, picnic, camp or do something!—in the wilderness itself. And they are soiling it and wearing it out! It happens at many a beach, river valley or desert.

A supreme example is the Grand Canyon, known world-wide for its pristine beauty. The sheer pressure of people, most of whom arrive by private car, is causing destruction of "things as they are." Wilderness trails are powered to dust by countless feet, campsites are soiled by the 14,000 people a year who float the river (yet up to 1948 fewer than 100 had done so); at access points, parking lots and buildings to meet tourists' wants and needs destroy the very isolation that is a key to the attraction.[4] We are ruining our own assets!

Gas guzzler and land gobbler

When we turn to fuel consumption we find that, taking one US gallon of fuel, an average car with one passenger achieves twenty passenger miles per gallon, a small car carrying four people ninety *pmpg*—roughly the same as a city bus—and a minibus with a full load of seven returns 175 *pmpg*.[5] Yet in the United States private cars are calculated as using 40% of the total oil burned each year,[6] a figure which is understandable when it is known that the number of cars in that country was growing twice as quickly as the number of people. Similar figures can be seen elsewhere. The great oil price hike in 1973 and subsequent oil shortage scares such as that caused by the overthrow of the Shah of Iran have done little to curb the car's thirst.

No matter how costly driving becomes through increases in the price of cars, fuel and repairs, we all keep and use our transport, cutting back on other expenses if our demands for higher wages are not met. Those at least were the findings of a New Zealand Ministry of Energy Committee after qualitatively surveying a sample of New Zealand motorists.[7] And these conclusions would seem to be confirmed by the growing worldwide popularity of cars in "developed countries" over the 1970s, despite the rising costs.[8]

Gas-guzzling energy rape is not the only worry. Another is the gobbling up of land. We are running out of space, yet we all know what happens in city after city. Previous patterns of settlement, social relationships and commerce (some good, some bad) are disrupted to build roads, freeways, underpasses, overpasses and massive parking facilities. The greatest consumption of land has been in cities such as Dallas and Los Angeles, which have used up 50% of their land area for roads and parking lots—basically for private cars. Other North American cities like Washington D.C.

and New York City are not far behind, with one third land space so far used.[9]

A mad impulsiveness in regard to the automobile seems to take over at times. Freeways demand to be built. I live in Wellington, the small but beautiful capital city of New Zealand. Its government, business and domestic areas cling closely together on steep hills and in narrow valleys, backing away from a basin harbor. The city clutches to the southern toe of the North Island. Beyond lies rough Cook Strait and then the South Island. But not long ago, at a tremendous cost of money, city character and emotion, a foothills' freeway was built to bring thousands more cars a day into the city: to go nowhere, to be parked mass upon mass in concrete parking facilities or in thin, crowded streets. There was protest, but in the end the car won the day, despite the fact that the freeway runs parallel to electric trains which have run that route for many years. Now thousands more motorists can come to work on their own four wheels, then share the common complaints of city traffic congestion and difficult-to-find, expensive parking.

There are unforseen effects when so much land becomes hard paved. One is water run-off, which becomes excessively large and rapid when little porous land is left to absorb rainfall. Another is who pays the maintenance? The answer, in one form or another in the mixed economies of the West, is the public purse. A third is wind build-up on the freeways themselves and around overpasses and underpasses near high buildings. And all of these things are more than trivial concerns. They affect the whole quality of urban life and city lifestyle.

A hurter of persons

Not long ago I knelt beside a gasping man in the middle

of a suburban road, in the misty gloom of a winter evening's homeward rush. The young pedestrian, who had charged into the path of a passing car as he left the railway station, died that evening. His wife of three weeks blamed herself—if she had been there, getting off the train with him before crossing the road, he would not have been hurrying home. He wouldn't have been so careless. She herself had intended to be on that train.

And the girl who drove the car? She had only held her driving license about a year. She had no chance of avoiding the dark figure which rushed in front of her foggy head-lights, but she will always remember the night she killed a man.

Only a few weeks later I stood for twenty minutes a little further up the same road. This time I was busy directing Saturday traffic until a traffic officer arrived, while other shoppers attended to a frail old lady. While crossing a busy intersection, she had been struck by the bumper of a car and flung into the air. The driver had simply been following other vehicles at moderate speed around a hard-to-see cor-ner. The under-twenty-five male driver had no chance of stopping. He sat dazed in his car for the next half hour. The young man killed, the old lady hurt—both were negligent.

But who were the real culprits? Neither they nor the drivers, but rather society collectively which sanctions by active participative consent conditions leading to appalling levels of accidents. All who drive add to the danger. Physical pain, shock, grief and guilt-stricken consciences which fol-low in the wake of accidents like these lurk behind every injury and fatality statistic we see.

Reading worldwide figures on road accidents is like being in a horror movie. Terror follows terror with almost nothing in between. The official New Zealand Yearbook records this comparative table of car accident, death and injury rates in

1976.[10]

Country	Persons killed	Persons injured	Killed per 10,000 vehicles	Killed per 100,000 pop.	Injured per 10,000 vehicles	Injured per 100,000 pop.
New Zealand	609	17,895	3.7	19.4	109.7	569.9
Australia	3,584	87,177	5.4	25.6	130.9	623.2
Great Britain	6,567	322,799	3.7	11.7	181.2	577.2

In Europe nearly 90,000 people are killed on the roads each year, with the number injured running at over 2,000,000. In North America as a whole the annual death toll is about 65,000.[11] And the figures show that private cars are the main person-hurters, with motorcycles making their significant contribution.

If similar levels of death or injury were caused by disease, there would be a public outcry against it, with strict emergency measures taken to combat the horror, inoculating it out of existence or destroying the pest which carried the plague. With the car a government merely orders another "drive safely" advertising campaign or strengthens the road patrols—measures which help, but which do not tap the root of the problem. To be fair, we must admit that a key difference is that disease has no demonstrable benefits other than population control, whereas the car provides a convenient service to individuals as well as relief for the public transport system. Also there is a large amount of economic investment in the car industry. One could hardly contemplate such an investment in disease!

"Drink" rather than cars is sometimes blamed for the road death and injury rates.[12] Assuredly if "drinking and driving" could be eliminated, accident fatalities would be dramatically reduced. But there are still overcrowding of vehicles, speeding, mechanical failures, bad weather and surface conditions, driver impatience or tiredness, passenger distraction, lack of skill and other other causes of accidents.

The car a hurter? It is in another more subtle way as well. It is a great breaker of relationships. Because I can get into a car and "go," I can always avoid the responsibilities and obligations of deepening kinship or friendship bonds. We can live on the other side of the city, even 100 miles away, and still see our aging parents. They are pleased when we come (though they may be pleased when we go—the children maybe are too noisy or our philosophies of life have grown apart), but are sad that seeing each other always has to be special and periodic, rather than ordinary and regular.

As we have already noted[13] a similar kind of thing happens in church when people come together by car, but don't live close enough to have frequent contact with each other. Relationships begun in and after Sunday worship are broken until next week. The cars zoom out, just as they zoomed in, honking to let everyone know that they love Jesus! So churches become big agglomerates, not smaller, more intimate followships.

"Wait a minute!" we may protest. "Surely the car is an initiator of relationship, a healer of hurt, by overcoming separation." Of course, that's true! But—and it's an extremely important "but"—a lot of the separation that makes reunion necessary would never occur in the first place, except for the ease of achieving it with the car. Suburban dispersity is based on the private car. It is not only families that want to be away from each other, but individuals as well. Indeed the car has become like a wristwatch—a necessity for every adult. The "family car" is no longer acceptable. One each is the contemporary demand![14]

Private technological worlds

It is more difficult to be certain about the more subjective areas, but these are equally alarming. Martin Pawley, whose writing we have glanced at already, suggests that the various danger and pollution statistics, such as those just noted, are chiefly useful as indexes of the enormous value which today's citizens place upon their cars:

> Today we buy cars because they are private techno-logical worlds ... about which we can worry and fantasize and hover and in the end dismiss—as me-dieval kings did their court favorites—in favor of new ones, exactly the same but different. It is only in such psychotherapeutic terms that short-life, unrelia-ble and dangerous automobiles make sense at all.[15]

And a few sentences further on, he comments:

> The confrontations with fear, danger and death that driving brings are uncommunicable private experi-ences, like the songs and masturbations of the bath-room. Bathroom and car are minimal spaces, somewhere between states, neither present nor absent yet infinitely possible, and it is in this technological approximation of the existential state of being that the charisma of the automobile is to be found. More than the freezer, the television set, the vacuum clean-er, the central heating and the air conditioning sys-tem, the automobile is the shibboleth of privatization, the symbol and the actuality of withdrawal from the community: the gift of wheels.[16]

Nonsense? Well, it's overwritten but, even allowing for that, the assertion is difficult to discount that for large num-bers of people the car is to a lesser or greater degree a private escape. It is also a means of extending desire and power beyond what can normally be achieved in everyday life.[17] Some people even seem to become different personalities when they drive. We might argue that for individuals to have psychotherapeutic opportunities is good but, granting that, is the cost of pollution, fuel, space and life worth it?

Even if we don't totally embrace Pawley's viewpoint, we can say in a more down-to-earth way that the car offers great privacy. To the extent that it does so, it is non-communal. Occupancy counts of cars going over a bridge or past a busy corner show that many carry only one person and that most are not filled to capacity, except during fuel crises or public transport strikes.[18] In a television panel about carless days occasioned by fuel shortages,[19] a friend of mine explained very convincingly how many interesting people he had met using public transport and how rewarding it had been for him since selling his car two years ago. To travel by public transport is potentially much more community-building. All tracks lead to the station at peak travel times, opening an opportunity for people to get to know those with whom they literally rub shoulders.

Of course a person has the right to choose whether to be private or public, silent or communicative, but at least the possibility is there. The sorts of contacts that the TV panelist made seem trivial, but in days of increased privacy in living and mobility of location it may be that, for some people, seemingly trivial relationships are vitally important for their general psychological well-being. For example, city bus drivers tell me that some old lonely people, bereft of relatives, ride the buses on their senior citizen passes, just to talk to people.

Social status

The same New Zealand survey to which we earlier referred shows that those surveyed thought of travel to work by car as an inalienable right. No matter how good public transport was, they would choose the car. Buses and trains are just too inflexible to bother with. Moreover "the ability to drive to work is a demonstration of social achievement."[20]

This latter point may be extended further. Monte Holcroft, in a beautifully written, most telling chronicle of driving in New Zealand, offers this anecdotal comment:

> I have found that people are often shame-faced to be without a car, as people were once ashamed to be seen abroad in patched or shabby clothing. Not long ago my wife and I went up to Cape Reinga and looked down upon Spirits Bay and the ghostly starting point around the rocks for the long journey of the dead to Hawaiki. We travelled by bus along Ninety-Mile Beach and through a swamp into which private motorists are not encouraged to venture. On the homeward journey we talked to fellow passengers at a stopping place outside the Wagener Museum, and could not help noticing how often conversation began with a reference to cars they had left outside their motel units at Kaitaia. Once it had been established that they were bona fide motorists, slumming briefly in a bus with tourists, they were relaxed and friendly. The center of snobbery, which appears to be ineradicable in human nature, has shifted generally from family connections to money; and the money-symbol today is a motor car, large and shining and expensive.[21]

If that's true—and I think it is—perhaps we ought to be

more than a little sad. A polluter, a fantasizer, a land gobbler, a killer has become all large, shiny and heroic!

Solutions and developments

Although the car is demonstrably the agent of a great deal of danger, grief and difficulty, it is probably the most highly sought consumer durable. Most social interpreters therefore see little likelihood of persuading John and Betty Citizen to voluntarily go without a car. Sociologist Wayne Youngquist, quoted in a commentary upon the May '79 gasoline cutbacks in the USA when people sometimes fought each other in long gas lines, said:

> The car is American's magic carpet and it gives people freedom and autonomy—it's their little box where they have control over their environment. There is resistance to anything that threatens the use of the car.[22]

"Exert economic pressure. Let the car owner bear full cost of his roads. *That* will make him sit up and take notice" is a commonly suggested answer. The motorist is not doing that in most places at the moment.[23] Road works usually come out of the public purse and are a tax on all, car owners and non-car owners alike, with road freight carriers in some countries being levied additional amounts. Take off what is in effect a subsidy, add it to car purchase price, registration and insurance, and the car might well be taxed right out of the market. Or would wage demands simply escalate? If "a car at any price" is the common insistence, wages certainly would. In any case where is the democratically elected government which would dare to so attack the constituency which elected it?

"Let the car disappear with the disappearance of fossil

fuels" is another solution, but by then a tremendous amount more accident, pollution, land space and personality damage will have been done.

Despite acknowledged difficulties some suggestions for change have been deliberate, bold, imaginative and well-prepared. As long ago as 1972, Goldsmith, Allen, Allaby, Darull and Lawrence, the architects of *A Blueprint for Survival*, together with an extensive list of other scientists who agreed with them, proposed a comprehensive political solution for Britain—"political" because it depended upon government planning, decision and enforcement. Ruling the existing situation as unacceptable for the sorts of reasons we have already discussed, they said:

> *It is clear that broadly-speaking the only alternative is public transport—a mix of rapid mass-transit by road and rail. Rail especially should never have been allowed to run down to the extent that it has. The power requirements for transporting freight by road are five to six times greater than by rail and the pollution is correspondingly higher. The energy outlay for the cement and steel required to build a railway, and the land area necessary for the former, is estimated to be four times more than for the latter. Public transport whether by road or rail is much more efficient in terms of per capita use of materials and energy than any private alternative. It can also be as flexible, provided it is encouraged at the expense of private transport.*
> *This is the key to the provision of a sound transportation system. First the vicious spiral of congestion slowing buses, losing passengers, raising fares, losing more passengers, using more cars, creating more congestion etc. must be broken. A commitment to*

> *build no more roads and to use the capital released to*
> *subsidize public transport would be an excellent way*
> *of doing this.* [24]

Farsighted? Utopian? When published, these and the other proposals contained in the blueprint aroused all over the world a great deal of serious reaction—and they still should. They have a logic about them, if not a popularity, which is difficult to dispute.

Three short diversions

Three other associated matters must be mentioned to complete a skeletal outline of the situation we confront with the car in the future.

The first of these has to do with pollution by exhaust gases. We have already seen this to be a serious problem. Can emission be cleaned up to render it innocuous? Probably it can.[25] The technology both for refinement of fuel and for making passifying devices to fit cars is available. It is already being used in the United States and Japan and it will get better. Provided governments insist on manufacturer and citizen response, the air poison "negative" for cars, still relevant now, will become less significant.

As an associated point, what about "alternative energy" cars? All sources seem agreed that what is awaited is a breakthrough in battery technology, because electric cars seem to have by far the greatest potential. What is needed are lighter batteries, giving longer life for greater distances with greater power flexibility to provide for vehicle acceleration. But again most sources are sure that the break-through will come. We could find ourselves with more cars than ever before, but nobody knows when.[26]

The second matter is the debate over how long fossil fuels, particularly oil and gas, will last. Experts disagree, and it's easy enough to see why. "Estimating oil reserves is like guessing the number of beans in a jar—only the jars are very deep underground and you aren't even sure exactly where they are hidden."[27] And that's not the end of the difficulty. How much of the reserves are practically and economically exploitable is another question, especially in relation to oil shale deposits.

Then there is perplexity over estimating future consumption. This estimate depends on many variables, including political uncertainties, the rate of development of alternative energy sources such as wind, sun, tides, thermal steam, energy farming and more hydro-electric power. Some experts say the supply of oil will fail to meet demand during the 1980s, but others postpone that crisis until the first or second decade of the twenty-first century.

One can go on collecting varied opinions, but futurologist Edward Cornish probably summarized the situation as well as anyone could, when he said in 1977:

> *Unless offset by improved technology, the depletion of fossil fuels may pose one of the most urgent problems of the next few decades; the loss of these supplies can very likely be offset by new and improved technologies and changes in lifestyles, but not without alteration of long-standing habits and industries— and such will not be effected painlessly.*[28]

The third diversion brings us once again to the "technological revolution". Will an information society develop so that mobility can be greatly reduced? Will people really stay put more, while all manner of information is screened in front of them? Who can tell? One scenario says "Yes"; another says "No". And the "No" can be either "No, it won't develop" or "Yes, it will develop, but mobility won't decrease.

This last version says, "Cars will only change their purpose from going to jobs to going to play and to alternative work". Some futurist forecasters think the changes will only apply to a small section of the population. Other believe these will spread to everyone, just as private mobility has done.

What do these three diversions say to us about the car? Could we guess that cars in most Western countries will be exhaust-clean by the early or mid 1980s, that fuel expense and shortage (both manmade and natural) will severely limit driving by the late 1980s, but that electric car and alternative fuel development will facilitate and further it by the mid 1990s as production plants revamp? And the information revolution? No violent changes before the 1990s—just gradual change leading to job redundancy and a decreased level of business mobility, while retaining the current level of leisure mobility?

Predicting is hazardous. The only reason for trying to guess the close future here is to prevent an unexpected situation sneaking up on us.

The car: is there a Christian view?

Impatient questions are probably surfacing as this discussion proceeds. "What has all this to do with Christian faith?" "Does this sort of issue have any place in a discussion about living in God's kingdom in today's world?" We will try to answer these questions in a number of ways.

Faced with some serious threat to health and life, Christians normally are amongst those who try to contain the threat and relieve misery. Confronted by an epidemic, Christians would usually urge and provide both preventative and curative care. Challenged by an education need, Christians would aim to find teachers. Christians have usually been at the fore through the helping professions in needy situations or causes. Is not the car a disease of endemic proportions? Is there not an educative task in demonstrating how to live? Ought not the Christian to be taking a lead and implementing remedial action? Surely the answers to these questions are all "Yes".

A Christian is to love God and to love his neighbor as himself.[29] No one who claims to inherit eternal life can dodge that. Yet we have in this matter of the ownership and use of the private car a case where "loving my neighbor" may be incompatible with my perpetuating the status quo. My neighbor is going to be hurt—even if he has not been yet—by accident, fuel squander, pollution, land abuse or psychological and sociological insularity. The method of hurting is more distant than hitting him with my fist or shooting him with a gun, but it is no less drastic in the long-term.

No follower of Jesus can overlook the commands to be salt and light,[30] which demand that God's love and truth be dispersed amongst the shortcomings of this present age. Where there is a social evil, such as the private car, we have a major responsibility for shedding some light and rubbing some salt. The private car a social evil? The economist E. J. Mishan calls it "one of the greatest . . . disasters that ever befell the human race".[31]

We have already noted that not all agree with this view. Many regard their cars as personal assets—flexible expressions of liberty and freedom, certainly not evil. But on the basis of what we know about the present and the near future, the Christian has to make a choice. Isn't that choice clear? I think it is. The negative side of the balance sheet stacks up so strongly that, at best, the car is a necessary evil—where "necessary" is defined by the tightest criteria. The car is certainly not a possession to be coveted or a toy to be droolingly admired.

At the personal level the Christian could fit an exhaust cleaner to a smaller model car (bought to conserve fuel) and use the car less—not at all in the city where it is only a clogging agent. He or she could drive more carefully to use less fuel and avert collision. These sorts of measures will help—significantly.

Then, of course, owning and using a car very little may bring its own conclusion—that it's not worth having one at all. Personal economy, or a sense of stewardship, may persuade us that having thousands of dollars locked up in a car which seldom turns its wheels is not a worthwhile capital investment. An even better alternative may be for Christians to lead the way in withdrawing from private ownership of cars altogether and press for alternative transport systems, urging a style of life which demands less mobility.

Going without

The thought of not having a car commonly produces a reaction like this: "How *could* I do without one? I couldn't possibly manage to . . ." Then follows a list of all the things for which the car is currently used.

Life without a private car, or without aspiring to one, is best contemplated as part of a total way of life whose elements are closely knit, derived from a specifically Christian approach to life. To answer "How could I?" let's pick up some earlier aspects of our discussion.

First, the question of place in relation to *mobility* arises. Knowing that I will be dependent on public transport, I may need to move, particularly as we have already observed the need for Christians to live near each other—to "live in the church" and "minister in a given place". Alternatively I may drastically reduce my use of a private car to short trips between my residence and the nearest boarding point for public transport, looking to non-car ownership as the longer term aim. And I may consider pressing by letter writing, personal advocacy, conversation and any other means for a major shift in society, away from private transport to more communal systems of transport—rail, buses (electrified for preference), taxies, rental vehicles, dial-a-bus services, rickshaws and pedal rickshaws, bicycles, malls, walkways and any other suitable alternatives—even where this means an about-face in public policy and expenditure.

This may mean advocating unpopular policies such as heavily taxing cars and transferring money so earned to the support of rail. It may mean opening ourselves to ridicule and criticism before our local government members or in letters to the editor. We will welcome on their merits some technological advances—such as those which enable people to stay in one place and information to travel—but oppose others which result in waste, consumerism or depersonalization.

Second, a Christian attitude to *time* will come into play. Insofar as the private car confirms an emphasis upon time's linear dimension and the consequent activism of rushing from event to event, we will reject it. The ability to move fast constantly encourages people to forget God's emphasis upon "the time in which they have been placed", by enabling them to hurry on to something else a few miles away.

Third, the car's consumption of fuel and capital is hardly in line with a life of Christian *simplicity* in days of world disparity between the affluent and the poor. On fuel consumption figures alone we are clearly pointed to service vehicles or, as an intermediate measure, towards some type of shares ownership—one car amongst four families perhaps.

There is another related point. Lester Brown, noted writer on population, food supply and related matters, says:

> *As countries turn to alcohol distilled from agricultural commodities as a fuel for automobiles, more and more farmers will have a choice of producing food for people or fuel for automobiles.*

And again:

> *For the first time since agriculture began, the world is faced with a massive diversion of agricultural resources to the production of non-food crops.*

If Brown is right, Christians could find themselves guilty by association—by an unthinking participation in an extremely far-reaching hurt to the poor. Brown envisages the sutiation developing whereby the choice will either be food or fuel. Somebody will miss out! Brown concludes:

> *. . . the decision to channel foodstuffs into the production of automotive fuel will inevitably drive food prices upward. The stage is set for direct competition between the affluent minority, who own the world's automobiles, and the poorest segments of humanity for whom enough food to stay alive is already a struggle.[32]*

Christian simplicity in regard to the car may no longer remain a personal option, but may become a moral necessity.

Fourth, we have already noted that the car is an agent for selfish *privacy*. And it is equally clear that as a *technical means* it often dominates the scene, in that people use it just because it's there. Indeed, this is just another example of "do because we can". The "can" eventually, over one or two generations, becomes the accepted norm. There is no question any more of whether or not it's "good". We have established a new, socially expected behavior:

> *I don't know what you do about this at the guy-in-*

> *the-street level. I think he is just swept along by an*
> *inevitable tide of social demand. We all use the ve-*
> *hicles (cars) because we have to use them. We can't*
> *really change . . . There is nothing we can really do.*
> *It is really just an inevitable fact of life and you*
> *have to resign yourself to it . . .[33]*

What terrible resignation! For this motorist "can" surely rules, even though he wishes it didn't. It is precisely this kind of social inevitability which Christians are equipped to overcome because they serve a king who is Lord of all. What an opportunity for Christians to lead the way!

Lastly, for *work* and *leisure* the car also can become too important: in our jobs as a reason for earning more and in our leisure as an agent of too much movement.

It should come as no surprise that various aspects of all the topics we have so far discussed come into view when we focus on the car, for it is truly a symbol of our life in the West today. For someone who wrestles through the matters of privacy, work, leisure and all the rest, rejection of the private car as a desirable feature of daily life is neither surprising nor difficult. Indeed, my own experience and observation of others so far shows that a large number of the things for which a car seems essential are either not important, or are more manageable without a car than had previously been thought—particularly if one is prepared to put aside the instant gratification of every want.

Possible exceptions

But surely there are some occasions when it is legitimate to say "I couldn't manage without a car". What about people who use their cars quite deliberately in Christian service? A lady I know drives all over the city (and beyond) bringing help and encouragement by her visits. There are many such examples. What is an appropriate policy for such circumstances? The answer is twofold.

Given the present situation, she and others like her should continue visiting. If necessary, a congregation might own two or three shared cars especially for those who carry out this kind of wide-ranging ministry. What we need to guard against is using this valid need as an excuse for total private ownership and use.

But second, churches in particular localities should take over as many of these functions as possible. The necessity for such dispersed visiting is a reflection of the failure of the local church to understand its neighborhood role. It has been all too willing to concede to mobility. Travel to evangelistic crusades on the other side of town or even in another city; purchase of homes in "the best areas", combined with too ready a willingness to drive miles to "a good church" if there's not a suitable one in the area; the "one-man ministry" where one individual covers a large area rather than encouraging ordinary Christians who live there to develop various pastoral gifts—all these are further symptoms of the uncritical acceptance of private car mobility.

Why be bothered?

Another objection takes this form: "I'm only one person—what's the use of my doing anything anyway? Everyone else drives!"

This is a very plausible objection because, if all take notice of it and nobody does anything, then of course nothing will be done! But Christians in "the post-Christian West" are still a sizeable minority and if all or many "did something", the effect would certainly be noticed. In addition, the church as a corporate body is more than the sum total of its adherents. If as a whole it moved in the direction of less mobility, the move would be heeded by society at large—or at least observed. Taken now, such a move would help to prepare people for the painful change to a world depleted of fossil fuels.

If by voluntary reduction the demand for cars lessened very significantly, there would be industrial changes. The car industry would be forced to adjust its long-range planning and output, even to the kind of car produced. To turn labor, expertise and capital from making cars to making railway locomotives and rolling stock is one other obvious yet far-reaching "adjustment" which could be made.

We do need to be realistic. The institutional church has not a very good track-record in opposing national evils, abuses or injustices. In the past it all too often has allied itself with the forces of oppression. The church in pre-war Germany did not see the danger in Hitler and the policies of the Third Reich until 1933–34, after Hitler had become Chancellor. By then a large part of the ecclesiastical machinery had been taken over by the State under the banner of the "German Christians". Only the "confessing church", stating its creed in the Barmen Confession and led with inspiration by Niemoller, Bonhoeffer and others, saw the truth and spoke it—at the cost of many lives.

Similarly the English church of the late 18th century saw no evil in the slave trade. That was an institution upon which the wealth and status of the British Empire rested. Slavery was challenged at first not by the church as such, but by a group of evangelical churchmen led by Wilberforce, Thornton and others, abused by their opponents with the derisive name "the Clapham Sect"—Clapham being the name of the village where they all worshipped. In the end their fight was successful, but what a fight it was. It lasted from the mid 1780s until March 25, 1807, when an abolition bill was passed in the House of Commons. It continued on a wider world scale until the Act of Emancipation was passed in 1833. All this demanded total dedication and commitment from the men of Clapham and others who later joined them.

Can one compare the private motor car with Hitler or the slave trade? It does sound absurd. A red BMW sitting in the driveway under an overhanging tree looks suitably attractive, while a sleek Mercedes looks positively enticing! There is a danger in overstating our case. Nevertheless, when we think of the extent of car-caused misery in our societies and look at the human dimension to the chilling statistics of road deaths and injuries, how can we avoid concluding that something is amiss? The slave trade and the Nazis beguiled the public of their day. Could it be that the car is doing the same to us, albeit more subtly?

Even if one is the only person convinced of our need to give up all private cars in the future, there is no need for him or her to back off. John Taylor, author of Enough is Enough, writes:

> It is not enough to say these things; our world is waiting for concrete examples ... We have to opt out of the drift and help one another to live in cheerful protest against it. We must not wait for all Christians to be persuaded of the need for this, neither should we waste our time designing a single rule of life for those who are so persuaded.[34]

Bishop Taylor is of course speaking about our entire affluent lifestyle. He is not addressing himself specifically to the affluence of private car ownership—nor may he want his comments to be so specifically applied. But what he says is pertinent to the question of the car. If we boldly accept his line of argument, we will not worry about being alone or apparently causing little effect. We will happily do what we can. Perhaps we will start by taking some of those measures already instanced or by cutting our annual car mileage from 10,000 to 5,000, then lock up our car for a trial period of two months with a view to going permanently without. It is only as people take that sort of action that there will be any lively demonstration for others to examine.

A discipleship that challenges and costs

We need to be clear about what is being advocated. The abolition of all motor vehicle transport is not in mind, only severe reduction. As technological research continues, we can hope for more efficient electric cars and the utilization of other alternative sources of energy. Special cases must be allowed too. The doctor, if he or she is to visit patients, certainly needs a car. Those involved in necessary trade, agriculture, transport or emergency services will need a variety of vehicles.

But the pleading of special cases must not be allowed to stand as an objection to the main case, which in essence is the elimination of the private car. We must be careful not to allow particular difficulties or graduations of necessity to invalidate the main contention. While confronting such an issue such as the car is not "the gospel", it follows *from* the gospel. It becomes a natural consequence of living as Christians—of being the new pilgrims.

We are essentially needing to show our calling—to be visible and articulate manifestations of God's kingdom now. One of the areas which confronts us happens to be mobility, and the car is its tangible symbol. We haven't chosen this issue; it is thrust upon us by the way people live and society has structured itself. We have been caught in a car-dominated way of life and we need to redirect ourselves to new living patterns.

Must Christians wait until change is forced upon us by

fuel exhaustion, urban decay or government restriction? If so, we offer no distinctive witness. We are but living in conformity to society around us. Rather we should be in the vanguard of reform, both to be true to our King and, as we have been commanded, to serve others.

Epilogue

A danger emerges when we examine a particular piece of society—as we have just done in chapter 8—even when we are careful to treat it as a symbol of deeper issues. The danger is simply this: that we become so enmeshed in the pros and cons of the particular case, that we drift away from the basic debate. For that reason, in concluding this book, I want to return to the central thesis, namely that the church is culturally imprisoned and that what is urgently required are escape routes to better ways—routes which yet stay firmly in society of which the prison is a part.

The problem is that the majority of us don't want to escape because we are so happy with conditions in the prison. Or worse, we are so inured to it that we don't realize we are inside! In either case we have to develop a real urgency, a strong sense of motivation, to shake loose at all! For me as a Christian that urgent motivation comes from biblical imperatives.

Time and time again, as I reflect, I am drawn to see that the angel of God, speaking to the church of Laodicea in Revelation 3:14–22, was addressing a situation which, in essence, closely paralleled our own. From being well taught and firmly established in Paul's time, as implied in the Letter to the Colossions, the Laodiceans had become, thirty years or so later, lukewarm, like the water which flowed into their city from hot springs outside. They earned one of the heaviest condemnations in Scripture: "I will spew you out of my mouth". Was their sin doctrinal error? No! It was cultural take-over. They had drawn into their lives the culture of the day in terms of wealth ("I am rich"), position ("I have prospered") and possessions ("I need nothing"). Cultural osmosis had almost conquered them.

The remedy? "Be zealous and repent." Accept God's reproof. That he is willing to reprove is a sign of his love. The Laodiceans were to put on purity ("gold refined by fire"), righteousness ("white garments") and truth ("salve to anoint your eyes that you may see"). And if we agree that we fit their mold, we will do the same. This repentance is to be accompanied by our re-invitation to the Lord to come into the church. He is outside knocking at the door. But there is also a great encouragement. Just as this lukewarm church attracts strong condemnation, so it calls from God a tremendous promise—that those who conquer the great temptation to be culturally absorbed "will sit with me on my throne"

All of this is strong meat and often we do not like it. Who wants to be told they are lukewarm, only fit to be discarded? I don't! And I don't suppose anyone else does. Repentance is not much in favor either—it has a nasty ring about it. Admittance of wrong and the consequent need to put that right is not a pleasing prospect. Yet all this is pertinent to this issue of the church's cultural imprisonment.

We have talked together—you as reader and I as writer—about some, but by no means all, of the features of our cultural bondage and what alternatives we might adopt. And we have seen that, if we are Christ's people in this world, our concern will flow out to others who do not share our faith, leading us to fight evil in every guise. But we are not to be just voices of protest or examples of escape. Rather we are to show an alternative way of living! We will be pilgrims, but pilgrims who stop to care. Flamboyancy is not asked of us, but the words of Jesus are unmistakably graphic:

> *You are the light of the world. A city set on a hill cannot be hid. Nor do men light a lamp and put it under a bushel, but on a stand, and it gives light to all in the house. Let your light so shine before men, that they may see your good works and give glory to your Father who is in heaven* (Matthew 5:14–16).

No Laodicean imprisonment is envisaged here!

We need to be sure that there is a distinctive city or light to be seen at all! That is why Christians must be concerned with leisure, work, mobility and all the rest. We dare not absorb uncritically all the characteristics of society around us. The city which shines is a pilgrim city. Christians are to live in God's kingdom—in his city—in this world. God's light is to shine and his city stand forth. In the new technological society his people are the new pilgrims.

Notes

All Bible references are from the RSV unless otherwise stated.

Introduction

1 Jacques Ellul, *The Presence of the Kingdom*, tr. Olive Wyon, The Seabury Press, New York, 1967, p 146
2 Ellul, p 148
3 John 13:35
4 Matthew 25:40
5 Luke 10:26–28
6 Luke 10:29–37
7 e.g., Hebrews 11:13
8 R. T. France, *The man they crucified*, Inter-Varsity Press, London, 1975, p 120.
This book is, I think, one of the very best available on the life of Christ. Simply written to suit a general reading public and therefore readably brief, it is based on deep theological insight into the Gospel texts, and on a comprehensive appreciation of the interrelationship of Jesus' life and teaching.

Chapter 1: Time

1 Genesis 8:11, Matthew 13:30, 1 Samuel 18:19, Luke 8:13, Acts 3:19 etc
2 Genesis 1:14
3 Deuteronomy 28:12, Jeremiah 33:20, Psalm 1:3, Proverbs 15:-23 and Job 5:26
4 Daniel 2:21 and Acts 1:7
5 Ecclesiastes 3:5

6 Lamentations 2:1

7 Isaiah 34:8

8 2 Peter 3:8, Psalm 90:4

9 e.g. Luke 4:5, Acts 14:3, 2 Corinthians 16:7

10 e.g., Matthew 26:18, Acts 1:7, Ephesians 5:16

11 e.g., Psalm 104:27

12 e.g. Jeremiah 51:6

13 John Marsh, "Time, Season", in Alan Richardson (ed.), *A Theological Word Book of the Bible*, SCM Press, London, 1950, pp 258ff

14 Mark 5:22–43

15 John 7:8

16 John 4:7–42

17 e.g. Mark 1:35ff

18 John 19:30

19 Psalm 34:1

20 Marsh, p 264

21 Acts 1:8

22 Timothy 4:2

23 Matthew 5:13

24 e.g. Matthew 13:40

25 e.g. Mark 10:30

26 e.g. Galatians 4:1–3

27 e.g. Mark 14:62

28 This is discussed briefly in E. Trocmé, "Time (Times)", in J-J Von Allmen (ed.), *Vocabulary of the Bible*, Lutterworth Press, Guildford and London, 1958, p 425. A fuller but readable discussion can be found in George Eldon Ladd, *The Gospel of the Kingdom*, The Paternoster Press, London, 1959, pp 32–33. Matthew 19:13–30 is a key synoptic passage.

29 e.g. Hebrews 6:5

30 Trocmé, p 426

31 1 Corinthians 12:4–30

32 Acts 15:28

Chapter 2: Simplicity

1 Luke 12:15

2 Martin Pawley, *The Private Future*, Thames and Hudson,

Great Britain, 1974, Pan Books, London, 1975, p 59

3 See chapter 6 (Work)

4 See "Living in the church" in chapter 5 (Mobility), pp 111ff

5 See especially chapter 4 (Means and ends)

6 Proverbs 6:6ff

7 1 Timothy 5:8

8 Matthew 6:2–18

9 Matthew 5:3–12

10 Vernard Eller, *The Simple Life, The Christian Stance Toward Possessions*, Hodder and Stoughton, London, 1974, p 117

11 Eller, p 119

12 Arthur G. Gish, *Beyond the Rat Race*, Herald Press, USA, 1973

13 Ronald J. Sider, *Rich Christians in an Age of Hunger*, Inter-Varsity Press, USA, 1977. An English edition containing figures, facts and illustrations pertinent to Britain is also available, Hodder and Stoughton, London, 1978.

14 Matthew 21:17, Matthew 26:6, Luke 10:38 and Matthew 8:14

15 Luke 10:4

16 John 12:14

17 Matthew 12:9–13

18 Luke 18:9–14

19 Matthew 26:26, John 6:32–35, Mark 2:22, Matthew 13:33, Matthew 16:6, Mark 8:23, Matthew 22:15–22, Luke 15:8–10, Matthew 21:18–22, Mark 13:28–29, Luke 6:43–45, Luke 13:6–9 and Matthew 13:3–23

20 Matthew 10:16

21 Matthew 18:20

22 Sider, p 189, IVP (USA) edition

23 That many churches are rich can certainly be documented by listing real estate (both capital value and annual earnings) and by setting out details of other investments, but to do so here would be so unfairly pick on one or two examples.

23 I realize defendants will argue that assets and income are wisely used, and that property held is a responsibility to be maintained and services in trust for others. But those contentions are made within an affluent framework, the whole of which is being

challenged.

24 Matthew 6:19–20 (NEB)

25 Bloesch, Jackson and Clark (see note 30, chapter 3) contain many examples.

26 Acts 4:34–35

27 The aim of Paul's interchurch help was equality, to be achieved by reciprocal giving. It's a point modern Christians overlook. See 2 Corinthians 8:10–15, especially versus 13–15

28 Luke 12:18

29 Jacques Ellul, *The Presence of the Kingdom*, tr. Olive Wyon, The Seabury Press, New York, 1967, pp 149–150

30 The church in Corinth

31 John Court, in talks to TSCF Conference 1975 and more fully in private conversation with the author both then and in 1979.

32 1 John 3:16–18

33 Genesis 2:15

34 Exodus 16:19–21

35 Harry Blamires, *The Christian Mind*, S.P.C.K., London, 1963, pp 3–4

36 Blamires, p 4

37 John V. Taylor, *Enough is Enough*, SCM Press, London 1975, p 65

38 Isaiah 61:1–3

39 Galatians 5:22

40 Ephesians 5:19

41 Mime, dance and some drama and their place in worship are considered seriously, with many practical illustrations, in Anne Long, *Praise Him in the Dance*, Hodder and Stoughton, London, 1976.

42 Matthew 25:40

Chapter 3: Privacy

1 The student residence at the Central Institute of Technology, Heretaunga, New Zealand, provides one of the best architectural and administrative recognitions of this loneliness and the need to overcome it that I have seen. Private rooms afford study privacy, but they are grouped in small "communities" around

facilities and common areas and the student government is organized representatively from that basis.

2 e.g. R. P. Penningroth and G. Tourney, "Recognizing and Determining the Meaning of Anxiety", *Postgraduate Medicine*, 46, No. 1, July 1969

3 "The Shut-out Generation", *Time*, 14 November, 1977, p 16

4 e.g. Martin Pawley, *The Private Future*, Thames and Hudson, Great Britain, 1974, Pan Books, London, 1975

5 e.g. John 2:2

6 e.g. Luke 5:29

7 e.g. Mark 4:10

8 e.g. Matthew 16:15–17 and 22–23

9 e.g. Luke 9:18

10 e.g. Luke 9:28, Luke 5:16, Mark 7:24

11 e.g. Luke 6:12–16

12 e.g. Mark 6:46

13 e.g. Matthew 6:6 (Phillips)

14 This is a favorite Greek Orthodox interpretation. See for instance, Chariton Igumen, *The Art of Prayer*, tr. E. Kadloukovosky and E. M. Palmer, Faber and Faber, London, 1966.

15 e.g. Matthew 26:36–46

16 e.g. 1 Kings 3:8

17 e.g. 1 Corinthians 1:19

18 e.g. Philippians 2:1

19 e.g. 1 John 1:3

20 Bruce Milne, *We Belong Together*, Inter-Varsity Press, England, 1978, p 33

21 e.g. Romans 12:6, Acts 4:32, 1 John 3:17, 1 Corinthians 12:28–30, 1 Corinthians 12:26, 1 Peter 4:9, Philippians 1:8, Galatians 6:1–2, Ephesians 4:3, James 2:2–4, Ephesians, 2:14, Acts 13:2 and 1 Thessalonians 3:9

22 John 15:12

23 Luke 18:18–23

24 *Ekklesia*, his usual word for church, meant an assembly of people called together. It was the common Greek word taken over by the early Christians and given a distinctive meaning.

25 1 Corinthians 12:12–30

26 See chapter 7 (Leisure), especially pages 150–151

27 Ephesians 2:19–21, 4:11–12 and 16

28 Milne, p 16

29 C. S. Lewis, *Fern-seed and Elephants and Other Essays on Christianity*, ed. Walter Hooper, William Collins, Glasgow, 1975, p 18

30 A brief introduction to Protestant ventures in community life is Donald G. Bloesch, *Wellsprings of Renewal*, William B. Eerdmans Publishing Company, Grand Rapids, Michigan, 1974.
    A useful practical handbook, based largely on American experience is Dave and Neta Jackson, *Living Together in a World Falling Apart*, Creation House, Carol Stream, Illinois, 1974. A comprehensive British book is David Clark, *Basic Communities*, SPCK, London, 1977. These three books, each from a different theological perspective, together provide a good introduction to the whole subject and its literature.

31 e.g. Sojourners Fellowship, publishers of *Sojourners*, published monthly in Washington, USA

32 e.g. The Emmaus Community, Langeweg, Netherlands. See Andrew Lockley, *Christian Communes*, SCM Press, London, 1976, chapter 2.

33 For many varied examples, see Clark, chapter 6

34 One of the most written about is Church of the Redeemer, Houston, where many church members live in community and carry on ordinary occupations. See Michael Harper, *A New Way of Living* Hodder & Stoughton, London, 1973.

35 A reasonable short history is to be found in Charles J. Mellis, *Committed Communities*, William Carey Library, 533 Hermosa St., South Pasadena, Calif. 91030, USA, 1976.

36 See chapter 1 (Time), especially pages 29–31

37 Esphesians 6:4, 5:25, 5:22 and 6:1

38 1 Corinthians 1:2ff

39 Lewis, pp 11–17

40 Tony Wilson (ed.), *The New Zealand Computer Society, Newsletter No. 86*, September 1978, PO Box 2788, Wellington, pp

3–4

41 Romans 12:4–8

42 For an interesting survey using both biblical and traditional sources, see William Barclay, *The Master's Men*, SCM Press, London, 1959

Chapter 4: Means and ends

1 See Chapter 8 (The car: a symbolic case study)

2 See chapter 2 (Simplicity)

3 Ephesians 5:18–20

4 At Christian leadership courses I have been to, we have often had periods of silence—either as a group or as individuals. Many people find these periods of inactivity very difficult to cope with. They do not know what to *do!* They show symptoms of restlessness and disturbance, e.g. going frequently to the toilet, returning to their rooms for something forgotten, shuffling in their seats, opening and closing books, frequently blowing their noses. Asians (from more reflective and meditative traditions) at the same course have never shown the same difficulties.

5 Psalm 46:10

6 Ellul, p 69. See Introduction, note 1.

7 The literature from which these labels are taken is diverse. A difficulty about following the developments here being described is that, because the changes are so rapid, any bibliography is out of date before it is used. Probably the best way to keep aware of continuing developments is to scan the contents page of:

   (a) The weekly news magazines—*Time*, etc.

   (c) Periodicals concerned with futurism—as these studies are beginning to be called, e.g. *Futures*

   (d) "House" magazines like *Telesis*, the journal of Bell, Canada.

8 Peter Goldmark, "Tomorrow We Will Communicate to Our Jobs", *The Futurist*, April 1972, p 56

9 W. J. Megaw (ed.), *Prospects for Man: Communication*, The Center for Research on Environmental Quality, Faculty of

Science, York University, Toronto, 1977, p 105

10 Jib Fowles, "No Future for Futuristic Communications?", an abstract in *Technological Forecasting and Social Change*, 8, 213–216, 1975, pp 214–15

11 Sir Ieuan Maddock, "Beyond the Protestant Ethic", *New Scientist*, 23 November 1978, pp 293–94

12 Peter Manning, "The Fascinating Shape of Your Future", *The Bulletin*, June 29, 1974, Cover Story

13 e.g. "A House That Thinks for Itself", *House and Garden*, July 1976, Volume 48, No. 7, p 52

14 Ellul, p 79

15 e.g. Mark 10:45

16 These matters are discussed from a slightly different viewpoint in "This age and the Kingdom now", see chapter 1 (Time), pp 30ff

17 See "A crucial modern issue: redundency" in chapter 6 (Work), pp 142ff

18 Matthew 5:16

19 Matthew 5:13

20 Some Christians may more readily accept the thesis of this chapter if we put it in the framework of the traditional distinction which the church has drawn between "in the world" and "of the world". "In the world" is good! That phrase sums up all the well-known imperatives about testifying to gospel truth. But "of the world" is bad.
The point is clearly made, for example in 1 John 2:15–17, that to be of the world—"world" meaning here corrupt society, not the created order—allows no place for love of God. To use technical means, without being dominated, is to be "in the world"; to use them, but be dominated by their self-generating dynamic is to be "of the world" and shut God out.

21 Sometimes people from other creeds, faiths and persuasions will join us because they, too, see the tyranny of means. We won't be afraid to co-operate with them, but will hold to our distinctive motivation because we want, above all, to be Christ's people, offering truth and love which stem from the cross and the resurrection, the dynamic for our social action.

Chapter 5: Mobility

1 Alvin Toffler, *Future Shock*, Pan Books, London, 1970, pp 76–77
2 Toffler, p 78
3 *Australian Year Book 1979;* p 80 gives population as 14,241,-500
4 *Australian Year Book 1979*, p 84
5 *Australian Year Book 1979*, p 84
6 Barbara Ward & Rene Bubos, Only One Earth, André Deutsch, London, 1972 p 144
7 Ward & Dubos, p 144
8 *Statistical Year Book 1977*, United Nations, New York, 1978, Table 163, p 567
9 *Statistical Year Book 1977, p 568*
10 N.Z. *Monthly Abstract of Statistics,* Dec. 79, p 13
11 *Australian Year Book,, 1979*, p 101
12 *Australian Year Book, 1979*, p 101
13 *Britian 1978*, an official handbook prepared by the Central Office of Information, London, pp 9–10
14 Toffler, p 76
15 David C. Thorns, *Suburbia,* MacGibbon & Kee, London, 1972, especially pp 127–131
16 Colossians 2:2, 3, 6 and 19
17 Acts 1:1
18 Ladd, pp 115–116. See chapter 1, note 28.
19 Barbara Ward, *The Home of Man,* André Deutsch, London, 1976, p 142
20 Acts 15:28
21 Genesis 2:8, 3:23
22 Genesis 37:2–47:1
23 Genesis 11:23
24 2 Samuel 5:5, 2 Kings 21:4, 1 Chronicles 6:32, Isàiah 52:1 and Matthew 23:37
25 Acts 1:4
26 Acts 16:9, 18:21, 21:4 and 27:23–24
27 Art Buchwald, The Tourist's Prayer, in *Los Angeles Times*.

(This "prayer" was given to me without any accurate references.)

28 See chapter 4, p 96

Chapter 6: Work

1 Genesis 2:15
2 Genesis 2:19
3 Genesis chapters 1 and 2
4 Genesis 3:17–19
5 Psalm 104:19–23
6 Exodus 20:9
7 e.g. 1 Samuel 17:15, Genesis 6:14–16
8 Proverbs 26:14–15
9 e.g. Mark 6:3. (The word *tekton* used here is not as precise as "carpenter", and strictly means "artisan" or "craftsman".)
10 Acts 18:3
11 Matthew 26:26–29
12 Luke 10:38–42
13 Luke 14:16–19
14 Matthew 10:3, John 3:1, Mark 1:19 and Acts 16:14
15 1 Thessalonians 4:10b–12 and 2 Thessalonians 3:6–13
16 2 Thessalonians 3:6 and 10
17 Colossians 3:22–25. (NEB) The other passages in the group are Ephesians 6:5–9, 1 Timothy 6:1–2, Titus 2:9–10 and 1 Peter 2:18–25.
18 Colossians 2:18—4:6
19 Colossians 3:18–19, 3:20–21 and 4:5
20 Allan Richardson, *The Biblical Doctrine of Work*, SCM, London, 1952, p 18ff
21 Richardson, p 19
22 Ecclesiastes 3:22
23 John 6:27–29
24 Matthew 26:10
25 1 Corinthians 3:4–9
26 1 Corinthians 16:10
27 Brede Kristensen, "Jacques Ellul: A Brief Sketch of His Work", *Christian Graduate*, Vol 29, Dec. 1976, p 109 (my

italics)

28 e.g. Luke 5:32, Romans 9:25, 1 Corinthians 1:9

29 e.g. Romans 15:15–20, 1 Corinthians 15:58, Philippians 2:25–30, Hebrews 6:10

30 Richardson, p 36

31 Ed. Diserens, "Call", in J-J Von Allmen (ed.), *Vocabulary of the Bible*, Lutterworth Press, Guildford and London, 1956, p 50

32 Jacques Ellul (quoting Luther), "Work and Calling", James Y. Holloway and Will D. Campbell (eds), *Callings*, Paulist Press, USA, 1972, p 24

33 Gustaf Wingren, *Luther on Vocation*, Mhulenberg, 1957, p 9. This book is probably the best sympathetic expostion of Luther's view.

34 Henri Perrin, *Priest & Worker, the Autobiography of Henri Perrin*, tr. Bernard Wall, MacMillan & Co., London, 1954, p 49

35 Perrin, p 52

36 e.g. Colossians 1:15–20, Romans 1:18–20, Revelation 19:16

37 The Puritans are frequently praised or blamed for developing the main characteristics of the modern work ethic, building on Luther, Calvin and other reformers. For a brief but clear discussion of this from a sympathetic commentator see Leland Ryken, "Puritan Work Ethic: The Dignity of Life's Labor", *Christianity Today*, October 19, 1979, pp 15ff.

38 Max Weber, *The Protestant Ethic and the Spirit of Capitalism*, Allen & Unwin, 1956; R. H. Tawney, *Religion and the Rise of Capitalism*, 2nd edition, Murray, 1948

39 Douglas Hyde, *Dedication and Leadership, Learning from the Communists*, University of Notre Dame Press, USA, 1966, pp 93–94

40 Udo Middleman, *Proexistence*, Hodder and Stoughton, London, 1974, p 26

41 Peter Wagner, "Confessions of a Workaholic—a Christian Hooked on His Job", *Eternity*, August 1975, p 24

42 Luke 10:7. This text is really speaking of the propriety of a Christian ministering and being supported by the people to

whom he ministers, but it has often been extended to apply to all jobs.

43 Colossians 4:1

44 See "Some far reaching possibilities" in chapter 4 (Means and Ends), pp 96ff

45 International Federation of Commercial, Clerical and Technical Employees (F.I.E.T.), "Background Paper Prepared for Conference on Computers and Work, Vienna, November 1978" in Graeme J. Ogilvie, General Secretary, NZ Insurance Workers' Union, *New Technology—A Union Response*, 16.1, October 1979.

46 Ogilvie, p 10 (quoting 1978 Nora report, France)

47 Robots are even being used in Australia to shear sheep! For a survey of flexible automation (i.e. robots) and the effects, see Gene Bylinsky, "Those Smart Young Robots on the Production Line", *Fortune*, December 17, 1979, pp 90–96.
   This account quotes Joseph F. Engelbert, the founder of Unimation, a key firm in the field, as saying that robots may replace 5% of the Western world's blue-collar workforce by the end of the twentieth century. Some other commentators would say that was a low estimate.

48 For a short discussion of all the points in this paragraph, based on collation of many sources, see Rev. Roger Clarke, *The Microprocessor Revolution*, Church of Scotland, Home Board, 121 George St, Edinburgh, 1979, p 10.
   At the time of writing this book, Clarke's paper was one of the best short accounts available on the microprocessor revolution and its consequences.

49 Chapter 4 (Means and ends)

50 1 Corinthians 5:6

51 For instance, the communication of more information by a television-telephone link may save people mobility, thus reducing car clutter or airport congestion. Therefore we may well argue for such innovation in some circumstances. But in other situations regular personal meeting may be necessary for other reasons, and therefore a television exchange of information may not be desirable.

52 This fight may demand questioning of, and challenge to, some of the very structures of society. For instance we are right to ask questions about who should make decisions concerning use of resources, including labor. Queries may need to be put about transnational companies and their influence on people in a given place, when top level policy decisions are made, thousands of miles away from where the effects will be felt, by people who don't bear the effects and whose motive is profit for their shareholders. For example, one group whose pamphlet recently came across my desk says it has 250,000 employees in 78 countries spanning six continents, but with nearly all its shares held in one country. The power such a company has to influence markets, politics and people is considerable.

53 1 Peter 2:20–21

54 See chapter 1 (Time), p 29ff

Chapter 7: Leisure

1 Division of Social Responsibility, *Declaration of the Methodist Church on the Christian Use of Leisure*, Methodist Church of Great Britain, 1974, p 15

2 See especially "Work and calling" in chapter 6 (Work), pp 130ff

3 Talk to youth movement and missionary group leaders at Frederick Wallis House, Lower Hutt, NZ, August 1978

4 Gordon J. Dahl, "Time, Work and Leisure Today", *Christian Century*, February 10, 1971, p 185

5 David Bridge, *Looking at Leisure*, Epworth Press, London, 1978 p 22. His figures are from E. H. Phelps-Brown, *A Century of Pay*, MacMillan, 1968.

6 Walter Kerr, *The Decline of Pleasure*, Simon and Schuster, New York, 1962, p 39

7 Staffan B. Under, *The Harried Leisure Class*, Columbia University Press, New York, 1970

8 Mark 2:18–22

9 See especially pp 62ff

10 e.g. Exodus 20:8–11

11 e.g. Luke 13:10–17

12 Mark 2:27–28

13 Acts 20:7, 1 Corinthians 16:2

14 Matthew 28:1 and John 20:1

15 Luke 24:13ff

16 Mark 2:23–26

17 See the discussion (Preoccupation with work . . .) in chapter 6 (Work), pp 139–141
    See chapter 6 (Work), especially "Useless things", pp 128–129

19 Daniel Thomas Jenkins, *Christian Maturity and the Theology of Success*, SCM, 1976, p 82

20 Matthew 11:28

21 Luke 5:5

22 Matthew 11:29–30

23 See chapter 3 (Privacy), especially "With God privacy", p 74f

24 The writings of Anthony Bloom, Greek Orthodox Metropolitan in Great Britain give some insights into interior prayer, e.g. Metropolitan Anthony Bloom, *School for Prayer*, Darton, Longman and Todd, London, 1970

Chapter 8: The car: a symbolic case study

1 *NZ Official Year Book, 1979*, Department of Statistics, Wellington, p 312. Note 2.6 is the figure for both 1977 and 1978, having moved steadily from 2.9 in 1973. And 2.6 is not the lowest figure in the world!

2 Barbara Ward and Rene Dubos, *Only One Earth*, André Deutsch, London, 1972, p 100

3 This research has been done by R. R. Brooks, N. I. Brooks and others at Massey University, New Zealand. See especially R. R. Brooks, N. I. Ward and E. Roberts, "Lead Levels in Sheep Organs, Resulting from Pollution from Automobile Exhausts," *Environmental Pollution*, No. 17, 1978, pp 7–12.

4 W. E. Garrett, "Grand Canyon: Are We Loving It to Death?", National Geographic, Vol. 154, No. 1, July 1978, pp 16ff

5 Barbara Ward, *The Home of Man*, André Deutsch, London, 1976, p 142.

6 Ward and Dubos, p 100

7 McNair Surveys NZ Ltd, "A Qualitative Examination of the

Attitudes and Motivations of Private Motirists", *Ministry of Energy: Technical Publication No. 1*, December 1978/January 1979, pp 20–24, especially p 23.

(This research paper was prepared for The Energy Conservation Campaign Committee.)

8 For instance, *Australian Year Book, 1979*, p 454, records motor vehicles on register per 1000 population:

1972	1973	1974	1975	1976	1977
389.8	403.8	418.7	435.6	451.9	463.4

And 13,000 miles from there, *Statistical Abstract of Sweden 1978*, Vol. 65, p 199, shows on the same terms of reference:

1972	1973	1974	1975	1976	1977
302	307	323	336	350	346

9 Ward, p 143

10 *N.Z. Official Year Book 1979*, Department of Statistics, Wellington, p 319

11 Figures (approximated to round numbers) are taken from *Statistics of Traffic Accidents in Europe 1977*, United Nations, 1978, especially pp 8–9. This record gives individual European countries, a European total, and then North America as a comparison. (Population figures are also given to allow percentages to be estimated.)

12 The consumption of alcohol in connection with driving is in most countries a serious contributory cause of road accidents. *Drinking and Driving*, a report of a departmental committee of the Department for the Environment (UK) 1976, p 1, says: "Alcohol accounts for at least one in ten of all deaths and injuries on the roads and its share is growing".

A good survey of known research before 1971 is to be found in F. A. Whitlock, *Death on the Road* (Studies in Social Ecology and Pathology), Tavistock Publications, London, 1971, chapter 7, but should be complemented by reading such a paper as Donald C. Pelz and Stanley H. Schuman, "Drinking, Hostility and Alienation in Driving of Young Men", *Proceedings of the Third Annual Conference of the National Institute on Alcohol Abuse and Alcoholism, June 20–22, 1973, Washington, D.C.*, N.I.A.A.A., Maryland 20852, 1974.

13 See "Living in the church" in chapter 5 (Mobility), pp 111ff

14 A Qualitative Examination of the Attitudes and Motivations of Private Motorists, p 7

15 Martin Pawley, *The Private Future*, Thames and Hudson, Great Britain, 1974; Pan Books, London, 1975, p 52 (his italics)

16 Pawley, p 53 (his italics)

17 Frequently this is to vent aggression (see Petz and Schuman, note 12 above) or just to enjoy the sensation of speed which can't be gained any other way, e.g. A Qualitative Examination of the Attitudes and Motivations of Private Motorists, pp 17 and 30. For more detailed data see Meyer, H. Parry, *Aggression on the Road*, Tavistock Publications, London, 1968.

18 I have frequently occupied odd moments waiting at a bus stop or a street corner in NZ cities, by doing occupancy counts. For most times of the day, I find they come out at about 60% one person occupancy. Since fuel crisis publicity has been prominent, the percentage of one person cars has been lower at peak, "going to work" times.

19 "Carless days" is a NZ government scheme to restrict fuel consumption by requiring every car owner to nominate a day on which it is illegal to use that car. Stickers are displayed accordingly but exceptions are allowed.

20 A Qualitative Examination of the Attitudes and Motivations of Private Motorists, p 13

21 M. H. Holcroft, *Carapace*, John McIndoe, Dunedin, 1979, p 118 (his italics). The places mentioned are well-known scenic points at the northern tip of the North Island—places rich in Maori history. Holcroft's book is one of the very best I have read about the car. It deserves a readership well beyond NZ shores, because of its social insight into the car's place in our lives.

22 "Gas: A Long Dry Summer", *Time*, May 21, 1979, p 39

23 But a number of countries have partial taxes on sales of cars. These are steps in the suggested direction.

24 Goldsmith, Allen, Allaby, Darull and Lawrence, *Blueprint for Survival*, Tom Stacey, London, 1972, pp 68–69

25 See for instance statements in "Future World Trends", a *Brit-*

ish Cabinet Paper, 1976, p 14, section 44

26 For a brief survey of worldwide development of electric cars, see "An Open Road for the Electric Vehicle," *New Scientist,* Vol 78, No. 1098, 13 April, 1978, p 70.

For battery technique, see G. A. Weiner, "Battery breakthrough recharges electric auto", *Iron Age,* 221, April 24, 1978, pp 32–33.

A useful earlier document with special relevance to Australia is The Bureau of Transport Economics, *Electric Cars,* July 1974. (It also contains—in chapter 2—a strongly expressed defence of the private car of any sort and its place in modern society, on the grounds of flexible usefulness.)

27 Taken from "Guessing What's There", *Time,* May 8, 1977, p 5

28 Edward Cornish, *The Study of the Future: An introduction to the art and science of understanding and shaping tomorrow's world,* World Future Society, Washington D.C. 1977

29 Matthew 22:37–39

30 Matthew 5:13–14

31 E. J. Mishan, *The Conomic Growth Debate—An Assessment,* George Allen & Unwin, London, 1977, p 122

32 These four quotations are all from a Worldwatch Institute study on trends towards producing energy fuels from crops, extracts from which were published under the title "Fuel Crops Take Food from People", *The Dominion,* March 17, 1980, p 3.

33 A Qualitative Examination of the Attitudes and Motivations of Private Motorists, p 33. This is an extract from comments made by one of the motorists surveyed.

34 John V. Taylor, *Enough is Enough,* SCM Press, London, 1975, p 69